The Maine Collection

Portico of the McLellan-Sweat House
Photograph: Danielle Vagenas

Portland Museum of Art
Portland, Maine

The Maine Collection is sponsored by the Portland Museum of Art Guild. The Guild was founded in 1976 and is charged with the responsibility of creating and maintaining volunteer personnel to carry out projects and fund raising events to benefit the Museum. The Guild is also charged with promoting activities which increase the visibility of the Museum in the community. Its present committees include Art in Bloom, Young Friends, Luncheon Lectures and the Flower Committee.

Proceeds from the sale of this cookbook will go toward the restoration of the McLellan-Sweat House of the Portland Museum of Art.

Inquiries and orders should be addressed to:
The Maine Collection
Portland Museum of Art Cookbook
P. O. Box 6128
Falmouth, Maine 04105

| First Printing | June, 1993 | 10,000 copies |
| Second Printing | December, 1993 | 10,000 copies |

Printed in the USA by

WIMMER
The Wimmer Companies, Inc.
Memphis • Dallas

Table of Contents

From the Editor

Welcome to *The Maine Collection*, a celebration of Maine's culinary heritage. This cookbook includes recipes as varied as the people of our state. It embraces traditional foods which are still an important part of our lives as well as contemporary adaptations and new, creative dishes which are both healthful and easy to prepare. This exciting "collection" of recipes has been made possible through the vision and commitment of the Cookbook Committee and the hard work of the many dedicated volunteers who tested, proofread and edited the exceptional recipes found in this book. We are deeply indebted to them and to the many friends, Maine artists and inns from all parts of the state who submitted over 500 wonderful recipes. We regret that limited space does not permit the use of all of them.

The Committee is very pleased that the proceeds from the sale of this book will go toward the restoration and re-opening of the McLellan-Sweat House, the fine Federal period home which originally housed the Museum. This stately mansion and the adjacent L. D. M. Sweat Memorial Galleries, the magnificent 1911 addition to the Museum, have been closed to the public for ten years.

In the words of Henry Nichols Cobb of Pei, Cobb, Freed & Partners, and the designer of the 1983 Charles Shipman Payson Building, the McLellan-Sweat House gives to the Portland Museum of Art a "unique identity" and should be, along with the L.D.M. Sweat Galleries and the Payson Building, an

Façade of the Portland Museum of Art, 1983

Photograph: Steve Rosenthal

integral part of the institution, and that "all three buildings should together house the Museum's collections." Mr. Cobb envisioned "a Museum embodying in its own buildings — with a vividness unmatched by any other institution of its kind — the architecture and cultural heritage of the community it serves."

The Committee has worked to make sure that our cookbook's appearance and contents tie the past with the present and the old with the new — just as Mr. Cobb did so masterfully when he linked the Museum's three buildings by enclosing them with the handsome McLellan fence. We feel that this "unique" cookbook reflects the spirit of Mr. Cobb's concept of continuity and community.

We are pleased to present to you *The Maine Collection* and invite you to enjoy it and our very special Museum.

Tinker Barron
Editor

Committee

Editor — Tinker Barron
Assistant Editor for Design — D. Lombard Brett
Assistant Editor for Recipes — Mead M. Brownell
Treasurer — Cecile P. Carver
Consulting Editor — Jane Smith Moody
Wine Consultant — George Brett
Graphic Artists — Karin Lundgren, Lynne Averill
Editorial Assistants —
Gael McKibben, Cassie Simonds, Stan Sylvester, Lisa Witte
Marketing Director — Penny Ebberts
Marketing Assistants —
Deborah J. Fogg, Linda F. Laguerre, Cissie Lindemann, Jean Key-Maginnis

The Cookbook Committee would like to thank the following organizations and individuals for their generous support of *The Maine Collection*:

The Board of Trustees
The Museum Guild, Ann Willauer
The Friends of the McLellan-Sweat House
Barbara Shissler Nosanow, Director, Portland Museum of Art
Staff members and volunteers:
Eileen Arsenault, Lisa Austin, Michele Butterfield, Marilyn Dyhrberg,
John LaBrie, Alice Mary Pierce, Cynthia Thebault,
Ann Staples Waldron, Pam Webber

From the Director

High Street Elevation
Portland Museum of Art, 1980
Colored pencil: Laurie Olin, I. M. Pei & Partners

All of us in the museum world have undoubtedly had mentors in the course of our professional careers. One of mine — a man no longer with us, Dr. Joshua C. Taylor, former director of the National Museum of American Art at the Smithsonian Institution and William Rainey Harper Professor at the University of Chicago — always said, "Never trust an art historian who doesn't like to eat!"

Is there a natural symbiosis between the culinary and the visual arts? Since Dr. Taylor was my mentor in so many ways — a great director, art historian, and teacher whom I admired inordinately — I was always glad that in his judgment I had the minimal, requisite qualifications for the profession. He ate with gusto and discrimination, being both gourmet and gourmand. I hope I may live long enough to continue the tradition!

With that in mind, it is with great pleasure and pride that we bring you *The Maine Collection*. This Cookbook also celebrates our collection of paintings and decorative art objects — works by Homer, Bellows, Kent, Hopper, Marin, Zorach, Wyeth, and others as well as the superb Joan Whitney Payson Collection of French Impressionist and Post-Impressionist paintings. Our three buildings, presenting three important moments in the development of

American architecture, are also integral parts of our collection.

Thus, it is an added pleasure that the proceeds of the sale of the Cookbook will serve a great cause — the renovation of one of our buildings that is one of America's most distinguished examples of domestic architecture of the Federal period, the McLellan-Sweat House. I need sing no song of praise to the exquisite contours of its architectural moldings or the delicate neoclassical traceries that adorn its fireplaces. For those of you who have seen it — or carry a memory of it in your hearts from days gone by — it sings its own song. That its present state is one of sad nobility breaks the hearts of those who love and cherish it. It embodies Maine's past, and its future.

As you savor each of these recipes, rejoice with us that with each bite we are one delectable mouthful closer to the renovation and reopening of this House to the public. May we all live a thousand years to appreciate this treasure in our midst!

Barbara Shissler Nosanow
Director, Portland Museum of Art

From the Historian

Since 1908 the Portland Museum of Art has preserved one of Maine's great houses, the McLellan-Sweat House. Built in 1800-01 for merchant Hugh McLellan, the mansion was the residence of the McLellan, Wingate and Clapp families before its acquisition in 1880 by Colonel Lorenzo di Medici Sweat, a prominent attorney and politician. After Colonel Sweat's death in 1898, the house became the property of his widow, the noted author Margaret Jane Mussey Sweat.

A staunch supporter of the fledgling Portland Society of Art, Mrs. Sweat willed her home and estate in 1908 to the organization for the purpose of establishing an art museum in memory of her husband. Mrs. Sweat's wishes were fulfilled when John Calvin Stevens' handsome museum addition to the mansion opened in 1911 along with the house.

The McLellan-Sweat House was planned and constructed by the local archi-tect-builder John Kimball, Sr., as a major statement of Federal period architec-ture. Kimball's design has long been praised for its skillful balance of impres-sive size, graceful proportions, and intricate detailing. As early as 1859 Portland historian William Willis ranked it among "the best houses in the state of its time." More recently this has been affirmed in its designation by the Department of the Interior as a National Historic Landmark, one of only 34 properties in Maine to be accorded such distinction.

In all historic homes, renewal must take place periodically, and that time is now at hand for the McLellan-Sweat House. The proceeds from the sale of this very special cookbook will be devoted to the restoration of the mansion's great interior spaces. Accordingly, this volume should be on the kitchen shelf of all those who admire Maine's architectural heritage and the McLellan-Sweat House in particular.

Earle G. Shettleworth, Jr., Director
Maine Historic Preservation Commission

Stairway of McLellan-Sweat House
Photograph: Richard Cheek

Beginnings

Gate to L. D. M. Sweat
Memorial Galleries

Daddy Homer's Fourth of July Punch

This was Winslow Homer's younger brother, Arthur's, favorite recipe. He was the first Homer to come to Prouts Neck in 1875 on his honeymoon. He had a 4th of July party for all the members of the community, an opportunity to meet each other.

	Juice from 6 dozen lemons
	Juice from 6 dozen oranges
	Skin from 2 dozen lemons
6	quarts fresh strawberries, crushed (or frozen, if out of season)
3	pounds sugar
3	quarts water
3	quarts strong tea (16 bags)
1	small bottle lemon concentrate
9	large bananas, sliced
12	quarts New England rum

Boil tea bags and lemon skins in water for 30 minutes. Chill. Combine all other ingredients in stoneware crocks to mull for a week. Store, covered, in a cool place. Stir daily. On the 7th day, strain through cheesecloth and bottle. This is quite potent and should be served over crushed ice.

Makes 6½ gallons, enough for 135   Brad Willauer

Abbottson Eggnog

This recipe came with Mrs. William Widgery Thomas, Sr. from her family home in Baltimore, "Abbottson."

1	quart cream
6	eggs, separated
½	pint brandy
1	gill rum
6	tablespoons sugar

Beat yolks until light. Add sugar and stir in spirits, very gradually. Pour in cream. Beat the whites to a froth, then fold in.

Zella B. Thomas

Fish House Punch

Punch was very popular in the 17th & 18th centuries. This punch (Fish House), Mint Julep and Eggnog are the only punches that remain in today's culture.

1	pound sugar
1	quart fresh lemon juice
2	quarts rum
1	quart cognac
½	cup peach brandy

Dissolve sugar in the smallest amount possible of cold water. Pour in lemon juice. Stir in rum, cognac and brandy, in that order. Chill. Allow mixture to mellow for several hours, giving an occasional stir. Serve in punch bowl with an ice ring.

Serves 25

Souffléd Common Crackers

These, served with soup and salad, are different, popular and perceived to be less self-indulgent than rolls or muffins. They disappear!

12-ounce bag of Vermont Common Crackers, available at some supermarkets, as well as some fish stores and specialty stores
Ice water
Butter

Preheat oven to 500 degrees

Split 2 or 3 crackers per person and soak in ice water to cover until they are completely soggy (may take 20-30 minutes for some). Lift out carefully and drain on paper towel. Move to a lightly greased cookie sheet(s) and dot with butter. Bake at 500 degrees until puffed (about 10 minutes), then reduce heat to 375 degrees and bake until browned, about 45 minutes. Serve immediately. I often soak and drain quite a number at one time, then freeze on the cookie sheet. When solid, I place them in a plastic bag and later bake them as I need them, making allowance for frozen condition. Not microwavable.

Nancy Payne

Curried Walnuts

Different!!!

1	pound walnut halves
½	cup sugar
2½	tablespoons corn oil
½	teaspoon salt
¼	teaspoon ground cumin
¼	teaspoon coriander
½	teaspoon ginger
¼	teaspoon ground cloves
½	teaspoon chili powder

Preheat oven to 325 degrees

Blanch walnuts 1 minute in boiling water. Drain and toss with sugar and oil. Let stand 10 minutes. Arrange in single layer on rimmed cookie sheet. Bake 30-35 minutes or until nuts are brown and crispy. Put into bowl. Combine seasonings and toss with nuts.

Curry is a blend of various spices:
turmeric, cumin, coriander, fenugreek, red pepper
and the addition of other spices of personal preference.

Herb Curry Dip

A sure hit with crisp vegetables as the flavorful dippers.

1   cup mayonnaise or salad
     dressing
½   cup dairy sour cream
1   teaspoon crushed Italian herb
     mixture
¼   teaspoon salt
¼   teaspoon curry powder
1   tablespoon minced parsley
1   tablespoon grated onion
1½ teaspoons lemon juice
½   teaspoon Worcestershire sauce
2   teaspoons capers, drained

Blend all ingredients and chill well.

Adele J. Robinson
Chairman and Editor, Portland Symphony Cookbook

Smoked Fish Dip

I like smoked blue fish best but I have also used smoked mackerel and smoked trout.

2   fillets of fish, smoked (to equal
     1½ cups when mashed)
¼   cup fresh minced onions or
     scallions
1   tablespoon lemon juice
½   cup sour cream
     Ground pepper and salt to taste

Mash 2 fillets of smoked fish and carefully remove small bones. Mix all ingredients together. Serve on crackers.

Serves 8

Anne Woodbury
Robert Woodbury
Chancellor, University of Maine

Taco Dip

This recipe can vary. If you like a certain ingredient, use more of it. If you don't like a certain ingredient, don't use it. Enjoy!

	Small onion, chopped
	Head of lettuce, shredded
1	large tomato, chopped
1	can olives, sliced
	Red or green pepper, chopped
2	16-ounce packages shredded Cheddar cheese
2	8-ounce packages cream cheese, softened
1	pound hamburg
1	package taco seasoning
	Sour cream (for an extra topping if using taco shells)
	Nacho chips or taco shells
	Hot or mild taco sauce, 1 large jar (or 2 jars if you like a lot of sauce)

Combine and cook hamburg and taco seasoning, following the directions on taco seasoning package. Combine softened cream cheese with ½ jar of taco sauce. Mix until well blended. Spread softened cream cheese mixture on bottom of a pan. Put ½ of shredded lettuce over cream cheese mixture. Spread a layer of hamburg and seasoning over lettuce. Next, spread a layer of shredded cheese. Spread onions over cheese. Spread a layer of olives over onions. Next, spread a layer of tomatoes. After tomatoes, spread a layer of peppers. Keep layering until all ingredients are gone. Use leftover taco sauce for dipping. Use nacho chips to eat taco dip or place dip in taco shells.

Greg Welch
Artist

Gander Farm Crab Dip

Sensational! Serve with corn chips or Fritos.

1 8-ounce package cream cheese (whipped is easier)
2 tablespoons Hellmann's mayonnaise
1 tablespoon milk
1 6-ounce carton fresh crabmeat
2 tablespoons grated onion
2 tablespoons horseradish
⅓ cup slivered almonds (sauté in butter)

Blend cream cheese, mayonnaise, milk, onion, and horseradish in blender or food processor. Stir in crabmeat, place in casserole and sprinkle with almonds. Bake in 375 degree oven for 15 minutes.

Chipped Beef Dip

2 tablespoons butter
½ cup chopped pecans
1 8-ounce package cream cheese, softened
2 tablespoons milk
2½ ounces dried beef
1 cup sour cream
2 tablespoons minced onion
½ teaspoon minced garlic
½ teaspoon pepper
Salt, to taste

Preheat oven to 350 degrees

Melt butter and sauté pecans. Blend cream cheese and milk in bowl. Add remaining ingredients and mix well. Turn into lightly buttered casserole and cover with pecans. Bake for 20 minutes.

Mrs. Stuart Symington

Hot Artichoke Dip

1   8-ounce package cream cheese, softened
4   tablespoons Parmesan cheese
1¼ cups shredded white Cheddar cheese
1   egg
3   teaspoons Worcestershire sauce
1½ teaspoons Tabasco (or other hot sauce)
1   can artichokes, packed in water, drained and chopped
⅓   cup mayonnaise

Preheat oven to 350 degrees

Mix all ingredients very well and put into a greased ovenproof baking dish. Bake at 350 degrees for 25-30 minutes or until it puffs and is golden. Serve with Triscuits or toasted bread rounds.

Serves 6 to 8   Michele Butterfield

Smooth Fruit Dip

Nice with apples and baby carrots.

1   12-ounce container low fat cottage cheese
¾   cup drained, unsweetened, crushed canned or fresh chopped pineapple
1½ teaspoons vanilla extract
½   teaspoon cinnamon

Place all ingredients in processor or blender. Blend until smooth and creamy. Serve with sliced fruit or vegetables.

Marilyn Doe

Curried Crabmeat Pâté

It's good, quick and perfect for cocktails. You may substitute shrimp or lobster.

1   cup fresh crabmeat
½   small onion, coarsely chopped
½   cup heavy cream
6   tablespoons butter, softened
1   teaspoon curry powder
¼   teaspoon salt
1   teaspoon fresh strained lemon juice
6   drops Tabasco
    Minced parsley

Place crabmeat in food processor. Add onion and ½ cup of cream. Blend for one minute. Add remaining cream if too dry. Blend to a smooth purée (if it seems wet, don't worry; it will firm up in refrigerator). Cream butter with curry powder until smooth and fluffy. Beat it, little by little, into crabmeat purée, stir in lemon juice, Tabasco and salt. Spoon into crock, sprinkle with minced parsley, cover with plastic wrap and chill overnight or for at least 3 hours. Serve with toast or crackers.

Serves 4 to 6

Cornelia B. Baxter

Smoked Mackerel or Trout Pâté

This can be used as an appetizer or as an hors d'oeuvre. I try to keep some frozen at all times so as to be able to bring it out if unexpected guests arrive. It can be defrosted in the microwave defrost cycle, about 1½ minutes.

12   ounces smoked mackerel or trout
4   ounces butter, melted
4   ounces cream cheese
4   ounces cream

Flake fish and put in blender. Add melted butter and rest of ingredients. Blend to a smooth consistency. It is better made the day before and kept in the refrigerator. It may also be frozen. Serve with your favorite crackers or melba toast.

Serves 6 to 8   Anita C. Stickney

Black Bean Pâté

Fools guests every time. Tastes like an elegant liver pâté.

1	pound cream cheese
1	10½-ounce can black bean soup
¼	teaspoon ground thyme
⅛	teaspoon chili powder
¼	teaspoon onion powder
1	teaspoon salt
2	tablespoons Worcestershire sauce

Blend all ingredients until smooth. May be frozen.

Makes 2½ cups   Mrs. Widgery Thomas, Jr.

*Pâtés need to be given one
or two days to mature after making.*

Mushroom Mousse

Use as an appetizer with crackers.

½ pound mushrooms, sliced and sautéed
½ teaspoon gelatin
1 tablespoon sherry
¼ cup cold chicken broth
1 egg, separated
1 to 2 drops Tabasco
¼ cup mayonnaise
1 teaspoon capers
1½ tablespoons chopped onion
½ teaspoon lemon juice
½ teaspoon garlic salt
Pinch of white pepper
½ cup heavy cream

Beat egg white until stiff. Soften gelatin in sherry and broth in blender container for a few minutes. Blend briefly. Add all ingredients but cream and egg white. Blend again. Add cream and blend. Place in mixing bowl and fold in beaten egg white. Pour in mold and refrigerate at least two hours.

Serves 6 to 8

Salmon Mousse

Serve with green mayonnaise.

Juice of ½ lemon
2 tablespoons plain gelatin
½ cup hot chicken broth (chicken bouillon cubes)
1 pound canned salmon (remove skin and bones), drain, reserve juice

1 cup crushed ice
1 cup heavy cream
Juice from salmon

Place all ingredients in blender, cover and blend 20 seconds. Pour into 4 cup mold. Let set in refrigerator for at least two hours. Unmold and serve with green mayonnaise. Blend 1½ cups thick mayonnaise and a handful of chives, leaves from 4 sprigs tarragon and 4 sprigs parsley. Add grated rind of 1 lemon. Blend 30 seconds. Check for flavoring. Pale green is pretty and delicious on salmon mousse.

D. Lombard Brett

Caviar Mousse

A delicious cocktail party mold, best with black bread squares.

1 tablespoon gelatin
2 tablespoons cold water
½ cup boiling water
1 tablespoon lemon juice
1 teaspoon Worcestershire sauce
2 tablespoons mayonnaise
1 pint sour cream
¼ teaspoon dry English mustard
1 4-ounce can red caviar (Use more, if desired)

Soften gelatin in cold water. Dissolve in hot water. Add lemon juice and Worcestershire sauce. Blend well. In another bowl, blend mayonnaise, sour cream and mustard. Add gelatin. Stir in caviar, pour into 4 cup mold and chill well. Note: do not double this recipe.

Serves 6 to 8

Mushroom Cheese Spread

Believe me when I tell you it's delicious.

1 cup chopped mushrooms
1½ cups grated sharp cheese
½ cup mayonnaise
½ cup chopped green onions
24 slices party rye bread

Preheat oven to broil

Combine first 4 ingredients. Spread thin layer of butter or margarine on bread. Then spread mixture on bread. Place on cookie sheet under broiler until cheese melts. Serve immediately. Bread slices may be spread and refrigerated ahead of time.

Serves 8 to 12   Anne O. Jackson
                                                                      Trustee

Rum Raisin Spread

This is a special item I invented for my catering business. Serve with the best of crackers. Freezes well.

4 8-ounce packages cream cheese
½ pound bag chopped walnuts
½ box raisins, soaked overnight in port
  Brown sugar to taste
  Rum extract to taste

Blend cream cheese in processor until smooth in texture. Add all else and refrigerate overnight.

Makes 3½ pounds.   Susan Woodruff Brown

Herring Spread

A jar of Maine's marinated herring becomes a very tasty and snappy appetizer spread for the fish lover!

1   8-ounce package cream cheese
1   8-ounce jar herring pieces in wine sauce, drained
3   tablespoons minced parsley
¼   teaspoon dried dill weed
    Generous dash Tabasco sauce

Blend ingredients in food processor in order given. Mellow two or three hours before serving with toasted French bread, rye bread or crackers.

Serves 8 to 10   Barbara Y. Sturgeon

Hummus Bi Tahini

4   cups (about 2 cans) garbanzos (chick peas), drained
½   cup tahini (sesame paste)
⅓   cup warm water
⅓   cup olive oil
    Juice of 2 lemons
5   cloves garlic, chopped
1½ teaspoons salt
1   teaspoon ground cumin
    Ground pepper, to taste

Combine chick peas, tahini, warm water, olive oil and juice of 1 lemon in food processor. Process until smooth and creamy. Add garlic, salt, cumin and pepper to taste. Process and correct seasoning. Add juice of 1 more lemon. Refrigerate in covered container until ready to use.

Alice Mary Pierce

Brie with Sun Dried Tomatoes

1 pound Brie
2 tablespoons minced fresh parsley
2 tablespoons freshly grated Parmesan
4 sundried tomatoes, packed in oil, drained and minced (reserve 1 tablespoon oil)
6 cloves garlic, mashed to paste
Crackers

Remove the rind from the Brie with a sharp knife and put the Brie on a serving plate. In a small bowl, combine the parsley, Parmesan, tomatoes and garlic, add the reserved oil, and combine the mixture well. Spread the mixture over the Brie and let stand about 1 hour before serving.

Serves 6   Margaret Lawrence

Chile Egg Puff

Good as appetizers or breakfast or luncheon dish.

1 dozen eggs
½ cup flour
1 teaspoon baking powder
½ teaspoon salt
1 pint small curd cottage cheese
1 pound (or less) jack cheese, shredded
½ cup melted butter or margarine
2 cans (4 ounces each) diced green chiles

Preheat oven to 350 degrees

Beat eggs until light. Mix dry ingredients and add to eggs, along with cottage cheese, jack cheese and butter. Blend all until smooth. Stir in chiles. Pour into buttered 9" x 13" baking dish. Bake at 350 degrees for

35 minutes, until firm. Serve with tomato salsa and sour cream if you wish.

Serves 10   Mymie Graham
                    Editor and tester of Portland Symphony Cookbook

Gravlaks

A special way to serve salmon.

2   pounds fillets of salmon, sliced
    to fit together, skin left on
2   tablespoons sea salt
1⅓ tablespoons sugar
½   teaspoon white pepper
1   ounce dry sherry
2   tablespoons dry dill or 4
    tablespoons chopped fresh dill

Freeze halved fillets overnight. Thaw in refrigerator. Blend salt, sugar and pepper. Rub into surfaces of fish. Sprinkle liberally with dill and a little sherry. Place two pieces of fish together (one on top of other) and press with weight for an hour or so. Then refrigerate in covered dish for four days, turning twice daily. Drain excess liquid as it accumulates.

                                        Mr. & Mrs. Tor Westgaard

Cumberland Island Canapé

1   8-ounce package cream cheese
1   tablespoon curry
¼   cup sherry
    Chutney, chopped green onions
    and parsley

Combine ingredients and form a mound on a flat plate. Cover with chutney, chopped green onions and parsley.

                                        Nancy Stewart Demming

Artichoke Appetizer Simone

2 6-ounce jars marinated
artichokes, drain and reserve oil
3 scallions, chopped
4 eggs, beaten well
1 clove garlic, crushed
Dash Tabasco
½ pound sharp cheese, grated
6 Uneeda crackers, crushed
Salt and pepper to taste

Preheat oven to 325 degrees

Chop artichokes and set aside. Sauté scallions in one half reserved oil. Combine and blend all ingredients. Pour into well greased 8" x 8" pan. Bake for 35-40 minutes at 325 degrees. Cool before slicing into 1" squares. (May be reheated on cookie sheet. Freezes well.)

Hot Appetizer Pie

This recipe has been well received for over twenty years. Guests will taste it ...love it ...ask what is in it ...and look at you with amazement!

2 8-ounce packages cream cheese,
softened
4 tablespoons milk
½ cup walnuts, coarsely chopped in
food processor and set aside
1 5-ounce jar sliced dried beef,
finely chopped in food processor
4 tablespoons onion, finely
chopped in food processor
1⅓ cups red and/or green peppers,
finely chopped in food processor
⅛ teaspoon pepper
1 cup dairy sour cream

Preheat oven to 350 degrees

Blend cream cheese and milk. Stir in dried beef, onion, green/red peppers and pepper. Mix well. Stir in sour cream. Spoon into shallow baking dish or pie plate. Sprinkle walnuts on top. Bake for 15 minutes. Serve hot with assorted crackers.

Serves 15 to 20　　　　　　　　　　　　　　　　Joan Fowler Smith

Onion Tart

This is an appetizer and is one of the most popular first courses we do.

4　large Spanish onions (or Vidalia onions when in season), peeled and thinly sliced
10　tablespoons unsalted butter
　　Salt and pepper to taste
⅓　pound puff pastry (frozen may be used)
1　tablespoon whole grain mustard
3　egg yolks
¼　cup heavy cream

Preheat oven to 375 degrees

Melt the butter in a large skillet over low heat. When the butter is melted, add the onions and stir well to coat. Cover the skillet and cook over low heat for 10 minutes. Remove the cover, raise the heat to medium high, and sauté the onions, stirring occasionally, until tender and just beginning to turn golden brown, approximately 25 minutes. Season with salt and pepper to taste. Defrost the frozen puff pastry, roll it ⅛" thick. Place it in an 11" tart pan and crimp the edges. Line the pastry with aluminum foil and fill with dried beans or pie weights. Bake in 375 degree oven for 25 minutes. Remove the weights and foil. Spread the grain mustard over the bottom of the baked shell. Combine the egg yolks and cream with the onions. Pour the mixture into the prepared pastry shell. Bake the tart for another 30 minutes. Slice into 8 servings and garnish with chives (preferably with blossoms). Serve immediately.

Serves 8　　　　　　　　　　　　　　　　　　　Chris Sprague
　　　　　　　　　　　　　　　The Newcastle Inn, Newcastle

Apricot Glazed Chicken Wings

This an excellent appetizer or summer meal.

1	5-pound bag frozen, or same amount fresh chicken wings, cut in 2 sections. Discard wing tips
	Salt
	Pepper
	Flour
2	sticks butter
	Oil to cover bottom of frying pan
3	to 4 cans beef broth
2	12-ounce jars apricot preserves
⅔	cup yellow mustard
½	cup brown sugar

Chicken: flour wings and sauté in butter and cooking oil (for this amount of chicken, you'll probably need 2 frying pans) until golden brown on both sides. Add beef broth (don't add water to canned broth; add enough to frying pans to cover the wings). Cover pans and cook until juices run clear when pierced with a fork. Then remove with tongs and place them on foil-lined cookie sheets and pour glaze over them. Broil until well browned, turn wings, glaze and broil. The wings can be served hot or cold.

Glaze: in saucepan, cook 2 jars apricot preserves with ⅔ cup yellow mustard and ½ cup brown sugar until bubbly.

Danielle Vagenas

Mussels Au Gratin

This is a simple appetizer for 6 to be served in the dish from the oven. So delicious, you might have to prepare two dishes!

1	bag mussels, cleaned and scrubbed
1½	sticks butter

1 tablespoon garlic, grated
1 pouch grated Monterey Jack
cheese
Bread crumbs

Preheat to broil

Steam mussels until shells open. Discard one shell leaving mussels intact in shells. Remove the beard (fuzzy growth) and place in shallow baking dish. Melt butter combined with 1 tablespoon grated garlic (more if desired) and dredge generously over mussels. Next, place cheese on mussels (lots) and sprinkle with bread crumbs. May be refrigerated at this point. To serve, place under preheated broiler 10-12 minutes until hot, bubbly and beginning to brown. Serve immediately with crackers.

Serves 6   Patt Ebbett

Crab Melt

Makes great appetizers or hors d'oeuvres for a cocktail party if used with 3-4 inch diameter French bread.

1 8-ounce package shredded
Cheddar cheese
1 loaf French bread
½ cup butter
1 tablespoon lemon juice
1 tablespoon Worcestershire sauce
½ teaspoon garlic salt
1 6-ounce container fresh
crabmeat

Preheat oven to 350 degrees

Melt butter and cheese over low heat. Add lemon juice, Worcestershire sauce and garlic salt. Process in blender until smooth. In bowl, fold in crabmeat and mix well. Slice bread in ½ inch slices. Spread crabmeat mixture onto bread. Place on ungreased baking sheet. Bake for 15 minutes. Serve immediately.

Makes 20 slices   Sonja Orff

Toasted Pita

Here is a crunchy, versatile alternative to crusty bread which is well served and well received with soups, salads, entrées or as a substitute for chips with dips. Leftovers may be frozen in foil and reheated.

1 package of 6 regular, or 8 mini, Pita pockets
1½ sticks of butter or margarine, room temperature
Fresh (or dried) dill weed, finely chopped

Preheat oven to 300 degrees

Split pita pockets. Spread butter or margarine evenly over each piece. Sprinkle with dill. Place on ungreased cookie sheet. Reduce oven temperature to 225 degrees. Bake slowly for about an hour until golden and crisp enough to snap into smaller pieces.

Caponata (Cold Eggplant Appetizer) "à la Linda"

A wonderful cold appetizer or luncheon dish.

2 pounds fresh eggplant, peeled and cut into ½" cubes (8 cups)
½ cup olive oil
2 cups finely chopped celery
¾ cup finely chopped onions
⅓ cup wine vinegar mixed with 4 teaspoons sugar
2 minced garlic cloves
3 cups canned Italian plum tomatoes, drained
2 tablespoons tomato paste
6 large green (or black) olives, pitted, slivered
2 tablespoons capers
4 anchovy fillets, rinsed and finely chopped

Freshly ground black pepper, to
taste
2   tablespoons pine nuts
Salt to taste

Sprinkle cubed eggplant generously with salt and place in colander to drain for 30 minutes. Pat dry with paper towels. Heat ¼ cup of olive oil in large skillet, add celery and cook, stirring, for 10 minutes. Add onions and cook until tender and golden. Transfer all to bowl. Add other ¼ cup olive oil and sauté eggplant over high heat, turning and cooking about 8 minutes, until golden brown. Return onions and celery to skillet and add remaining ingredients, except pine nuts. Bring to boil. Reduce heat and simmer, uncovered, for about 15 minutes. Stir in pine nuts. Refrigerate until serving time.

Yield: 8 cups   Judy Ribeiro

Cheese Crispies

*These may be frozen and refrozen. They make a good company canapé.
Easy to make in a food processor.*

1   stick butter or margarine at
    room temperature
½   pound sharp Cheddar cheese,
    grated
1¼ cups grated Parmesan cheese
1   cup flour
    Dash Tabasco
    Dash Worcestershire sauce
    Dash cayenne
1   cup Rice Krispies

Preheat oven to 350 degrees

Blend grated cheeses in food processor with butter or margarine. Add flour and seasonings down the spout. Blend in Rice Krispies. Roll into log and chill for future use or pinch into marble-sized pieces, flatten and bake at 350 degrees for 15 minutes. Use, or freeze in small batches.

Makes 4 dozen

Curried Cheddar Chips

6   ounces sharp Cheddar
4   tablespoons butter or margarine
1   cup flour
1   teaspoon garlic salt
2   teaspoons curry powder
   A pinch of cayenne pepper

Preheat oven to 350 degrees

Grate cheese, mix with soft butter or margarine. Stir spices into flour and mix with cheese, making a paste. Shape into a long roll, about 1" in diameter and wrap roll well. Refrigerate for several hours or overnight. Cut slices about ¼" thick and place on cookie sheet. Bake at 450 degrees for about 7 minutes and serve hot.

Makes about 60 pieces   Joan Leslie

Cheese Straws

Good to have ready in the freezer for emergencies or when you're feeling lazy. Never any left!

     Pepperidge sandwich bread
½ to 1 cup melted butter
     Finely grated Parmesan cheese

Preheat oven to 350 degrees

Trim off crusts and cut bread in narrow strips. Dip in melted butter. Dip into bowl of grated cheese. Put on small cookie sheet and freeze. When frozen, place in plastic bag to keep. To serve, toast in oven at 350 degrees for about 7 to 10 minutes. Watch carefully.

Anne Hilliard

Easy Cold Soup

This is a wonderful cold soup. Everyone seems to love it.

1   large bar of cream cheese
3   cans consommé
1   tablespoon curry
    Parsley sprigs, chopped

Blend all of the above. Chill. Garnish with chopped parsley. This may be served hot, too.

Serves 6   Lisa Witte

Curried Apple Zucchini Soup

An appealing way to use the fall harvest.

2   tablespoons margarine
1   large onion
1   large apple, peeled, cored, chopped
1   to 2 teaspoons curry powder, to taste
4   cups chicken stock
2   cups diced unpeeled zucchini
¼   cup uncooked rice
½   teaspoon salt
1   cup milk

In saucepan melt butter, sauté onion and apple until soft. Sprinkle with curry powder and cook, stirring, for less than a minute. Pour in chicken stock and bring to a boil. Add rice, zucchini, salt and cook until tender, about 30 minutes. Pour into blender and blend until smooth. Return to pan and add milk.

Serves 4 to 5

Gazpacho

4 large ripe tomatoes
2 teaspoons garlic, minced
1 medium onion, chopped
1 medium cucumber, chopped
¼ cup red wine vinegar
2 tablespoons olive oil
½ cup tomato juice
¾ cup seedless grapes, halved
Fresh toasted croutons

Dip tomatoes in boiling water, skin and core. Put in food processor with all other ingredients except grapes and croutons. Blend and chill. Garnish with grapes and toasted croutons.

Serves 6

Walk In The Woods Soup

May be served either hot or cold and is perfect either way.

⅓ cup white wine
4 tablespoons butter
1 cup chopped onion
¾ pound fresh mushrooms, sliced
2 cups chicken stock
1 cup heavy cream
Salt and freshly ground pepper
to taste

Soak mushrooms in white wine 1 hour, stirring occasionally. Melt butter in soup pot and sauté onions until tender. Remove mushrooms from wine, reserve liquid and add mushrooms to onions. Season and cook, uncovered, over low heat for 15 minutes. Transfer wine into pot, add chicken stock and bring to boil. Reduce heat and simmer for 45 minutes. Add cream to desired consistency. Do not boil.

Serves 4 to 6
Ruth Kimball
"The Picnic Hamper," Camp Hammond, Yarmouth

Mock Lady Curzon Soup

A delightful gastronomic experience and so simple.

1   quart V-8 juice (even amounts of this and the other two juices)
1   quart orange juice
1   bottle clam juice
2   tablespoons curry powder
    Sour cream or yogurt
    Parsley for garnish

Toast curry powder in bottom of pot until it is brown but not burned. Add liquid. Bring to a boil and cook over medium heat for 5 minutes. Allow to cool, then chill. Serve with a dollop of sour cream or yogurt and finely chopped parsley.

Serves 6 to 8   Shirley Cole Quinn

Fresh Green Pea Soup

Original fresh pea soup. It is good!

2   tablespoons butter
4   or 5 scallions, chopped
3   small red potatoes (very small)
3   cups chicken broth
4   cups water
4   cups fresh peas, shelled
4   cups fresh garden lettuce
¼   cup fresh mint leaves
    Sour cream

Sauté scallions in 2 tablespoons butter until soft. Add the chicken broth, water and potatoes. Cook until potatoes are tender, partially covered. Add the peas and lettuce. Cook 10 minutes, covered. Add the mint. Purée in a blender. Return to pot. Serve hot with a dollop of whipped cream or cold with a dollop of sour cream.

Serves 6 (or 8 for first course)   Rebecca Hotelling

Pea Soup St. Julian

Serve hot with blueberry or cornmeal muffins, or cold with dollop of sour cream on top and French bread.

1 package dried green peas
1 package dried yellow peas
1 cup dry white wine
4 minced garlic cloves
    White pepper
    Salt

Soak peas overnight in water, following package directions. Next morning, place peas in large cooking pot. Cover with sufficient water to cook until peas are tender. Add water to cut thickening. Add ½ cup white wine and garlic. Stir until smooth. Add salt and pepper to taste. On second day, when reheating to serve, add ½ cup white wine. Whisk until smooth.

Serves 6   D. Lombard Brett

Skier's Soup

This soup improves with age.

5 bouillon cubes
5 cups water
1 pound hamburg
1 large onion, chopped
1 teaspoon chopped garlic
2 28-ounce cans plum tomatoes
1 16-ounce can kidney beans
1 cup rice, uncooked
6 carrots, chopped
6 stalks celery, chopped
½ pound mushrooms, sliced
    Parsley
1 teaspoon basil
    String beans, fresh or frozen

Simmer bouillon cubes in water in a large soup pot. Fry hamburg, add onion and garlic. Drain off fat and add to soup pot. Add tomatoes, including liquid, beans, rice, carrots, celery, mushrooms and basil. Simmer 4 to 5 hours, adding more water if needed. Add beans and parsley at the end.

Serves 6   Ann Willauer
President of the Museum Guild

Ginger and Cream of Carrot Soup

A good holiday soup.

¼	pound butter
1	large onion, chopped
8	garlic cloves, chopped
6	bay leaves
¼	cup fresh parsley
2	cups white wine
1	pound carrots, sliced
1	quart chicken stock
2	tablespoons grated ginger root
2	teaspoons curry
1	teaspoon ground cloves
1	teaspoon celery seed
	Dash nutmeg and dash cinnamon
1	quart half and half
1	tablespoon grated orange rind soaked in a tablespoon of sherry

Melt butter in fry pan. Sauté onion, garlic, bay leaves and parsley until onion is clear and soft. Transfer to a large saucepan. Add wine, carrots, stock and spices. Simmer over low heat, uncovered, for 1 hour. Purée soup in blender or processor. Strain through a fine sieve and return to pot. Add cream and reheat but do not boil. Adjust seasonings. Serve very hot, garnished with orange rind.

Serves 8   Elizabeth (Cheeky) Draper

Squash Soup

4 cups chicken stock
3 medium onions, chopped
3 cups buttercup squash (1 large)
1 cup cream
1 tablespoon butter
1 teaspoon curry powder
5 whole cloves
Parsley

Wrap the squash in foil and bake at 400 degrees for 45 minutes. Peel, seed and mash the squash. Cook onions and cloves in stock until soft. Remove cloves and add squash. Purée in a blender. Cook curry powder in a little butter. Add to the soup along with the cream. Blend. Let soup sit for about an hour to absorb the curry. Serve hot or cold. If served cold, thin with a little light cream. Garnish with parsley.

Serves 8

Fresh Corn Chowder

For a first course, you may purée this soup in food processor or blender and serve hot or chilled, topped with fresh basil.

1 cup corn, fresh or cooked, cut off cob (1 can cream style corn may be substituted)
1½ cups chicken stock or canned low salt chicken broth
1 large potato
1 medium onion
1 cup half and half or evaporated milk
½ cup milk
4 tablespoons butter
1 tablespoon chopped fresh basil or 1 teaspoon dried basil
Salt, black pepper and white pepper to taste

Chop onion coarsely, dice potatoes and cook in chicken stock until tender (10 minutes). Add corn, milk and butter. Bring to just below boiling. Add seasonings to taste. Serve in bowls topped with basil.

Serves 2 generously as supper dish
or 4 to 6 as first course

George J. Mitchell
U. S. Senate

Bear Island Light Soup

Bear Island Light Soup derives its name from Bear Island Light (the soup itself is not light but quite hearty), which signaled the entrance to Northeast Harbor from 1838 until its decommissioning in the late 1980's. It was known as a "family" light by the Light House Service since it was safe enough for the keeper's family to live on (unsafe lights, such as Boon Island, were "stag" lights). The comfortable, two-story keeper's house is the only one on the Maine coast with a gambrel roof, and it may have been here that the recipe originated, or perhaps the warm orange color was reminiscent of the glow of the oil lamp originally used in the lighthouse. This dish is still popular in the Asticou area, the site of the original village of Northeast Harbor.

1 pound fresh carrots, cleaned, scraped and diced
16 ounces chicken stock or 2 cans chicken broth (skim off fat)
8 ounces milk
2 tablespoons crystallized ginger
2 tablespoons Kikkoman Teriyaki sauce (a modern addition)
Chopped chives or parsley to garnish

Steam carrots for seven minutes or until tender. Meanwhile combine chicken broth, milk and ginger in saucepan and heat but do not boil. Put heated mixture in blender or food processor and purée until ginger is dissolved. Add cooked carrots to this mixture and purée again. Add teriyaki sauce and reheat if necessary. May be served hot or cold with above garnish. Stir before serving.

Serves 4

William D. Hocker
Miniaturist

Chicken Congee

A soup that can be a nourishing and delicious luncheon meal.

½ chicken, skinned and cut in small pieces
2 cloves garlic, crushed
1 small onion, chopped
2" fresh ginger root, peeled and sliced
2 tablespoons oil
½ cup rice
2 cans chicken broth

Sauté garlic, ginger and onion in oil. When ginger perfume is strong and onion is limp, add chicken pieces and sauté briefly. In a separate pot, boil chicken broth and add contents of sauté pan and washed rice. Bring back to a boil and simmer until rice has burst and chicken is tender, approximately 30 minutes. If congee is too thick, add a little more broth or water.

Serves 4 to 6   Peggy Rockefeller

Cucumber Soup Tarragon

2 medium size cucumbers
2 cups water
1 envelope chicken broth
1 teaspoon dried tarragon
½ teaspoon salt
1 tablespoon flour
1 tablespoon margarine
4 ounces sour cream (optional)

Peel cucumbers and halve them lengthwise. Scrape out seeds and cut in small pieces. Braise in margarine with tarragon and salt until well blanched. Dust cucumbers with flour and stir well over heat. Place in blender with chicken broth, water and sour cream. Adjust seasoning. Serve hot or cold.

Serves 4   Claudia Kinnear

Cauliflower Soup Vienna

Buttered croutons taste lovely with this soup when served hot.

½   head cauliflower
½   teaspoon salt
2   cups water
4   ounces sour cream
    Dash nutmeg
1   envelope chicken broth

Boil cut up cauliflower in lightly salted water until done. Place in blender with rest of ingredients. Adjust flavoring to taste. Serve hot or cold.

Serves 4   Claudia Kinnear

Cold Garlic Potato Soup

¾   cup finely chopped white part of
    leek, washed well and drained
4   large garlic cloves, chopped
    coarsely
1½ tablespoons olive oil
½   pound russet (baking) potato
2½ cups chicken broth
3   tablespoons heavy cream
2   tablespoons minced fresh chives

In a heavy saucepan cook the leek and garlic, with salt and pepper to taste, in the oil over moderately low heat, stirring, until the leek just begins to soften. Add the potato, peeled and cut into 1" pieces, and the broth. Simmer the mixture, covered, for 10 to 15 minutes, or until the potato is very tender. In a blender, purée the mixture in batches, transferring the soup as it is puréed to a metal bowl set in a larger bowl of ice and cold water. Let the soup cool, stirring occasionally, for 15 minutes, or until it is cold. Stir in the cream, the chives and the salt and pepper to taste. Makes about 3½ cups.

Serves 2 to 4

Luncheon Lecture Soup

This recipe is infinitely capable of change. Its charm is in variety.

1   pound beans (navy, kidney,
    white, etc.); can also use canned
    beans
    Ham bones, meat bones
    Celery and leaves, chopped
    Onions, chopped
    Bay leaf
    Garlic
    Spices: thyme, oregano, pepper,
    salt, etc.
    Kielbasa or other type of
    sausage, sliced
    Frozen vegetables or leftovers
    Tomatoes, fresh or canned

Just soak and precook any dried beans according to package directions. Add remaining ingredients and turn crock pot onto low for 10 to 12 hours.

Serves 8   Cecile Carver

Beef Barley Soup

Great on a winter evening. Serve with crusty bread and salad.

1   to 2 pounds soup meat and
    bones (worth looking for meaty
    soup bones from butcher)
1   bay leaf
1   clove garlic, minced
3   large onions, chopped
1   pound carrots, peeled and sliced
2   stalks celery and leaves, chopped
3   tablespoons chopped parsley
1   24-ounce can plum tomatoes
¾   cup barley
    Salt and black pepper, to taste

Simmer soup meat, bones, pepper, bay leaf, garlic and onions in water until tender. Remove bones. Add remaining ingredients and cook until tender. If thicker soup is desired, add leftover mashed potatoes or 1 raw potato, grated.

Cooking time: 2 hours

Serves 4 to 6

Bean and Basil Soup

This is a hearty, nourishing soup for a cold day. We like it served with crusty bread, a green salad and warm gingerbread for dessert.

1	cup dried beans
2	zucchini, diced but not peeled
1	large potato, diced
3	large carrots, coarsely chopped
1	red onion, studded with 6 cloves
2	stalks celery, coarsely chopped
2	large onions, coarsely chopped
1	large can tomatoes
1	bay leaf
2	cloves garlic
1	tablespoon dried basil
	Salt to taste
3	cups chicken or vegetable stock
3	cups water
2	tablespoons olive oil
2	tablespoons parsley

Soak beans according to directions. Drain and rinse. Put beans in 6 quart Dutch oven. Add stock and water. Bring to boil. Add vegetables, herbs and spices. Do not add olive oil or parsley. Bring back to boil, then simmer for 2½ hours or until beans are tender. Discard onion studded with cloves and bay leaf as soon as beans are cooked. Taste for seasoning. Serve immediately or refrigerate to reheat the following day. Let individual diners sprinkle olive oil and parsley on the soup and eat without mixing them in.

Serves 6   Muriel Zacharyr

Bread and Cheese Soup

6 cups chicken stock, homemade
  preferable
½ teaspoon freshly ground pepper
4 slices bread, toasted
4 ounces Gruyère cheese, shredded
  Salt to taste

Bring stock to a boil, add salt and pepper. Break toast into large pieces
and divide into four soup bowls. Divide cheese among bowls equally,
pour boiling stock on top and serve immediately.

Serves 4

Wild Rice Soup

*Wild rice is the seed of an aquatic grass which has for centuries been
harvested by woodland Indians who gather the grass by paddling a
canoe through shallow water. After threshing to loosen the husks, it is
placed in a winnow basket, tossed into the air where the wind blows away
the husks and the seeds drop back into the basket. Aromatic, hearty and
nutritious, this soup is a satisfying meal with toasted pita and a green
salad.*

1 medium onion, thinly sliced
4 ounces fresh mushrooms, sliced
3 tablespoons butter
½ cup flour
4 cups chicken stock
1½ cups cooked wild rice
1 cup half and half
¼ cup dry sherry

Cut sliced onions into quarters. Cook onion and mushrooms in butter
until onion is transparent. Add flour and cook over medium-low heat for
15 minutes, stirring occasionally. Add chicken stock and cook approximately 10 minutes until smooth. Add wild rice, half and half, and sherry,
stirring until thoroughly heated.

Serves 4 to 6

Cassie Simonds

Bean Soup

*Makes a large amount of mixed beans for future use. Each recipe requires
2 cups of mixed beans.*

Beans: 1 pound each pinto,
navy, lentils, great northern,
Jack, green pea, yellow pea,
black eyed, kidney, baby lima,
soy, red
¼ teaspoon pepper
2 teaspoons salt
1 ham hock
2 large onions, chopped
1 16-ounce can whole tomatoes,
chopped
1 clove garlic, minced
2 teaspoons chili powder
¼ cup lemon juice

Use 2 cups of mixed beans. Wash well and place in large kettle. Cover
with water 2" above beans. Add salt and soak overnight. Drain, add 2
quarts of water, ham hock and pepper. Bring to boil and simmer for
1½ hours or until beans are tender. Add onions, tomatoes, garlic, chili
powder and lemon juice. Simmer 30 more minutes, stirring occasionally.
Remove meat from ham hock, chop meat and return to soup. This
freezes well.

Yields approximately 2½ quarts   Mead Brownell

*Give packages of bean combinations
with the recipe for a present.*

Mushroom and Chive Bisque

½ pound fresh mushrooms
½ cup butter
¼ cup flour
¼ teaspoon dry mustard
2 cups chicken broth
2 cups light cream
⅓ cup minced chives
¼ cup sherry
1 teaspoon salt

Clean mushrooms and chop finely. In a large saucepan, melt butter and sauté mushrooms until soft. Add flour and mustard, cooking and stirring for minute or so. Add chicken broth and cook until thickened, blending with a whisk. Add light cream and chives, reserving some chives for garnish. Flavor with sherry and salt to taste. Serve hot or cold. A good garnish is a dollop of whipped cream and a sprinkle of chives.

Serves 6

Noreen B. Evans

*Put leftover salad and V-8 juice in a
blender and you've created a good gazpacho.*

Salads and Dressings

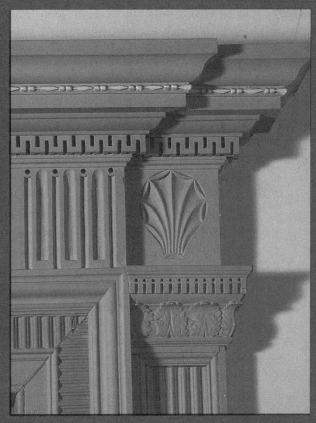

**McLellan-Sweat House,
drawing room mantle detail**

Cucumber Salad

3   cucumbers
¼   cup mayonnaise
¼   cup yogurt
1   teaspoon tarragon vinegar
¼   cup cottage cheese
¼   cup blue cheese, crumbled
     Pepper, freshly ground
     Red pepper for garnish

Cut cucumbers in half, lengthwise. Scrape out the seeds and slice. Sprinkle with pepper and toss gently. Mix remaining ingredients in separate bowl and blend very well. Fold into the cucumbers and toss thoroughly. Refrigerate until serving. Serve on green leaf lettuce with red pepper garnish.

Serves 4 to 5   Mary Haggerty
                        Lincoln House Country Inn, Dennysville

Fresh Broccoli Salad

A very easy, eye appealing salad. Can be made 3 or 4 hours ahead of time. It is colorful and very tasty. It always brings raves.

2   bunches fresh broccoli
10 slices bacon, cooked crisp and
     then crumbled
⅔   cup seedless raisins
2   onions, chopped
1   cup mayonnaise
½   cup sugar
2   tablespoons cider vinegar

Cook bacon until crisp, cool and crumble. Wash and cut broccoli into bite sized pieces. Combine broccoli, bacon, raisins and chopped onions into bowl in which salad will be served. In another bowl, combine mayonnaise, sugar and vinegar. Pour dressing over broccoli mixture and toss. Refrigerate for two hours before serving, tossing occasionally.

Serves 8   Anita C. Stickney

Easy Tomato Aspic

Simple and delicious.

1   1-pound can stewed tomatoes, chopped
1   tablespoon lemon juice
1   package lemon Jello
½   cup finely chopped celery

Scald tomatoes in saucepan. Add juice, Jello and celery. Stir thoroughly. Pour into attractive greased mold and put in refrigerator until set. Turn out on bed of lettuce and serve.

Serves 4

Rosy Tomato Aspic

2   cups tomato juice
1   tablespoon grated onion
1   tablespoon horseradish
3   tablespoons vinegar
    Pinch salt
1   large package red raspberry Jello

Combine first 5 ingredients and bring to boil. Pour over raspberry Jello. Put in mold and refrigerate until set and ready to serve.

Serves 4 to 6   Marilyn Spencer

Basil, Tomato and Bread Salad

This is truly a summer salad!

Red Wine Garlic Vinaigrette:
3   cloves garlic
½   cup red wine vinegar
1¼ cups olive oil
    Salt and pepper to taste

Place the garlic cloves and vinegar in the bowl of a food processor or blender, and blend. With the machine running, add the olive oil in a very slow, steady stream. Add salt and pepper to taste.

Salad:

2	large sweet red or yellow peppers, cut into 1" squares
6	slices good quality white bread, crusts removed
½	cup olive oil
3	large Italian plum tomatoes
3	cups chopped fresh basil leaves, washed several times and patted dry
1	medium cucumber, peeled, seeded and cut into ½" cubes
1	cup thinly sliced red onion
3	tablespoons grated Parmesan cheese
1¼	pounds fresh mozzarella, cut into ¼" cubes
¼	pound Parmesan or Romano, ungrated for shaving

Preheat oven to 450 degrees

Toss the sweet pepper squares with 2 teaspoons of the olive oil and roast in the oven on a cookie sheet for 7-10 minutes until slightly limp. Cool. Lightly brush each slice of bread on both sides with olive oil. Place in the oven on a cookie sheet until lightly browned on both sides. Remove from oven and cut into large 1" squares. Slice the tomatoes in half lengthwise and scoop out the seeds. Cut each half into 4 wedges. Place these ingredients in a salad bowl along with the basil, cucumber, onion, grated Parmesan and mozzarella. Add dressing liberally and toss. Let salad sit for 15-30 minutes so that the bread has a chance to soak up some of the dressing. Toss in more dressing just before serving, if desired. To serve, divide salad in the middle of 6 large plates. Garnish by shaving strips of the Parmesan with a vegetable peeler or cheese knife atop each salad.

Serves 6

Cheryl Lewis, Owner Chef
Cafe Always, Portland

Almond Orange Salad

An all time winner. Store no longer than 24 hours.

Dressing:
½ teaspoon salt
    Dash pepper
2 tablespoons vinegar
¼ cup salad oil
    Dash red pepper sauce
1 tablespoon snipped parsley

Shake dressing ingredients in tightly covered jar. Refrigerate.

Salad:
¼ cup sliced almonds
3 tablespoons sugar
¼ head lettuce
¼ head romaine
1 cup sliced celery
2 green onions (with tops), thinly sliced
1 11-ounce can mandarin oranges, drained

In a heavy frying pan, place the 3 tablespoons sugar and almonds over low heat, stirring constantly until sugar is melted and the almonds are coated. Cool and break apart. Store at room temperature. Tear lettuce and romaine into bite sized pieces. Place greens in a salad bowl, add celery and onions. Refrigerate until serving time. Five minutes before serving, add the well drained mandarin oranges. Pour dressing over salad, add the almonds and toss all ingredients together. Serve immediately.

Serves 4

Maryetta Bennett

Mixed Greens with Grapefruit, Fennel and Parmesan

8 cups of coarsely shredded romaine lettuce, rinsed, dried and crisped
3 cups of arugula or watercress or a combination, washed and dried (discard coarse stems)
3 cups of thinly sliced fennel bulbs
1 cup of thinly sliced radishes
3 ounces Parmesan, coarsely grated or thinly sliced (about 1½ cups)
3 large grapefruit or grapefruit/orange combination, peeled and pith removed, cut into 1" pieces

Combine ingredients in a large salad bowl and toss lightly. Serve with red wine vinaigrette dressing.

Serves 6 to 8   Peg Leavitt

If chives are hard to find, don't substitute dried, but use fresh scallion greens instead.

Cole Slaw

2   medium heads of cabbage, finely shredded (may add some purple cabbage for color)
2   medium white or purple onions, chopped
4   scallions, finely sliced
2   teaspoons salt
⅓   cup sugar
1   teaspoon dry mustard
½   cup cider vinegar
¾   cup vegetable oil
    Freshly ground black pepper to taste
4   heaping tablespoons light nonfat mayonnaise or salad dressing

Sprinkle cabbage with salt and let drain in a colander about 2 hours, squeezing as much water out as possible before continuing. May drain overnight if desired. Add onions. In a small bowl mix the remaining ingredients and stir into cabbage mixture. Adjust seasonings if needed by adding a bit of sugar first and, if necessary, more salt. Cover and refrigerate until ready to serve.

Serves 8 to 10   Barbara Bush

Chinese Coleslaw

Coleslaw:
1   medium cabbage, chopped finely
8   tablespoons slivered almonds, lightly toasted
8   ounces sunflower seeds, toasted (optional)
2   packages Ramen noodles (discard seasoning packet)
2   to 3 scallions, thinly sliced

Dressing:

2   tablespoons sugar
¼   cup vegetable oil
2   teaspoons salt
6   tablespoons rice wine vinegar

Crumble dry noodles, uncooked, into salad of cabbage, almonds and scallions. Put dressing in jar and shake. Toss salad with dressing and serve.

Serves 4   Sarah Marshall

Garlic Lovers Potato Salad

I encourage you to make this salad when your mint patch is getting out of control and when you plan to fire up a steak or sausages on your charcoal pit. You will only need firmly ripe, sliced tomatoes, salted and peppered, for a complete summer dinner of special significance, color and taste.

5½   pounds red potatoes, washed
8   cloves garlic, pressed
1½   cups very good olive oil
      Large bunch fresh mint leaves,
      washed and chopped
2   tablespoons coarse salt
1   tablespoon ground black pepper

Preheat oven to 350 degrees

Wash and dry red potatoes. Place in roasting pan. Bake in 350 degree oven for 2 hours. Wash and chop mint, set aside in refrigerator. Combine garlic, olive oil, salt and pepper in a small bowl. Set aside. Remove potatoes from oven. Let cool in pan 30 minutes. Cut potatoes into bite size pieces. Place in large bowl. Add olive oil mixture and mint, and toss. Cover with foil. Let stand at room temperature for at least 2 hours. Stir and serve at room temperature.

Serves 10 to 12   Cassie Simonds

Zoe's Potato Salad

Truly a family recipe. Excellent and easy. Super with hamburgers, steak or chicken.

12	small new potatoes, red or white
1	medium to large onion, very finely chopped
2	cups Hellmann's mayonnaise
	Juice of 1 lemon
	Salt and pepper to taste

Boil the potatoes until cooked but still firm, chill for 2-3 hours. Gently stir chopped onion into mayonnaise. Add juice of lemon. Place a 1 inch layer of thinly sliced potatoes in the bottom of round casserole or dish. Sprinkle with salt and pepper. Pour sauce over. Repeat the 1 inch layer of sliced potatoes, salt and pepper and thin layer of sauce. Finish with sauce on top. Chill for 3 or more hours. Tastes even better the next day.

Serves 6   Peg Dinan

Summertime Salad

1	pound pole beans, tipped and cut in 1 to 1½" lengths
1	clove garlic, minced
1	to 2 tablespoons olive oil
1	package Canadian bacon, diced
2	to 3 ounces feta cheese, crumbled
½	cup chopped walnuts, lightly toasted
2	cups tricolor "Radiatore" pasta, cooked as directed
½	cup sun-dried tomatoes in olive oil

Snip dried tomatoes, cover with boiling water for 2 minutes, drain well, cover completely in glass jar with olive oil and refrigerate. Put olive oil in cast iron frying pan, heat and add garlic. Then add green beans. Stir frequently over moderately high heat until beans are bright green. Add diced bacon and cook all until beans are tender-crisp. Stir frequently. Meanwhile, cook radiatore pasta as directed until "al dente" (do not overcook). Then drain well. Mix all ingredients together and toss gently in a large bowl. Serve at room temperature.

Serves 4

Faith W. Munson
The Stone Turtle, Little Deer Isle

Marinated Vegetables

Another good salad to take to a pot luck. Make vegetables and dressing ahead, then combine when ready to serve.

Salad:
4   cucumbers, scraped with fork and thickly sliced
4   peppers, red or green, cut into thick strips
4   large ripe tomatoes, cut into wedges
16 ounces white mushrooms, cleaned and halved

Dressing:
1   lemon
1   cup oil, olive or olive/canola blend
⅓   cup cider vinegar
2   garlic cloves, minced
2   tablespoons sugar
1   teaspoon salt
1   teaspoon coarse black pepper

Prepare vegetables in the order listed and place in plastic container with cukes on bottom, mushrooms on top. Make the dressing. Coarsely grate the lemon peel, then juice the lemon. Add peel and juice to remaining dressing ingredients and whisk. Let stand at least one hour and preferably overnight. About a half hour (up to one hour) before serving, pour dressing over vegetables. Put in serving dish and stir to coat. Stir about every 15 minutes until ready to serve.

Serves 8

Layered Vegetable Salad

This is an easy do-ahead winter salad.

1	cucumber, peeled and diced
½	cup vinegar
1	pound peas
4	stalks celery, diced
3	scallions, thinly sliced
¼	cup raisins
4	small carrots, peeled and diced
¼	teaspoon paprika

Dressing:

½	cup mayonnaise
½	cup sour cream
1	hard boiled egg, finely chopped
2	tablespoons Parmesan cheese
2	tablespoons seasoned salt
2	tablespoons parsley, chopped

Put the diced cucumber in a bowl and cover with vinegar. Leave for about an hour, then drain well. Cook the peas until just tender. Drain. Combine all the dressing ingredients and mix well. Place half the peas in the bottom of a glass serving bowl. Then add, in layers, half of each of the cucumbers, celery, scallions, raisins and carrots. Add a layer of half the dressing. Repeat the layering and end with a layer of dressing. Sprinkle the paprika over the last dressing layer. Refrigerate overnight or at least 4 hours.

Serves 6   Mead Brownell

Ducktrap Farm Smoked Trout and Rice Salad

Dressing:

3	cloves garlic
½	cup olive oil
½	lemon, juiced
1	teaspoon cider vinegar
1	teaspoon powdered mustard
	Salt and pepper to taste

Salad:

4 cups cooked rice
3 to 4 smoked trout fillets
2 cups chopped cooked celery
½ cup black olives, chopped
2 cups finely chopped carrots
1 medium onion, chopped
½ cup chopped parsley

Put all the dressing ingredients in a jar and shake. Set aside. Cook rice and allow to cool. Add celery, carrots, olives, parsley and onions. Flake trout meat into the salad. Dress the salad at least 1 hour before serving and chill. Vegetables may be marinated in dressing beforehand.

Serves 8   Laurie Lundquist

Hot Chicken Salad

To lighten up calories in this recipe, you may use light mayonnaise.

6 cups cooked, chopped chicken breasts
½ cup chopped onion
½ cup sliced celery
  Salt and pepper to season
1 teaspoon lemon juice
1 can chopped water chestnuts
1½ cups mayonnaise
2 cups shredded Cheddar cheese
  Potato chips, crushed

Preheat oven to 350 degrees

Combine all ingredients except cheese and potato chips. Mix well. Put into baking dish. Sprinkle with cheese, top with chips. Bake in 350 degree oven for 45 minutes or until casserole bubbles.

Serves 6   Maryetta Bennett

Curried Chicken Salad

This is a very good summer dinner served with a crunchy bread and a cake or fruit pie for dessert.

4 cups cooked chicken or 3 cooked breasts, diced
1½ cups mayonnaise
¾ cup chutney, your choice
½ teaspoon salt
½ teaspoon pepper
1 8-ounce can pineapple chunks
1 cup white grapes, seedless and sliced
1 6-ounce can sliced water chestnuts
1 cup melon, fresh
½ cup cooked bacon, crumbled
½ cup cashew nuts
1½ tablespoons curry powder
½ head leafy lettuce
1 large tomato, sliced and quartered for garnish

In large mixing bowl, combine and stir well the above ingredients except lettuce and tomato; let sit. Arrange chicken mixture on platter on bed of lettuce. Add tomato slices as decoration. Sprinkle with paprika or dill. Refrigerate for at least 1½ hours.

Serves 6 to 8

Cashew and Chicken Salad

Excellent summer meal.

4 boneless, skinless chicken breasts
1 package angel hair pasta
1 to 2 heads of lettuce
1 can salted cashew nuts
1 can mandarin oranges

Scallions, chopped
Sesame oil
Salt and pepper, to taste

Cut chicken to bite size chunks and cook in sesame oil in skillet or fry pan, stirring constantly. When cooked, remove from heat and chill. Prepare pasta and chill. In large serving bowl place washed lettuce. Layer pasta on top of lettuce. Place chicken on top of pasta. Sprinkle cashew nuts on top of chicken. Drain syrup from mandarin oranges, wash oranges with water and drain again. Place oranges on top of cashews. Sprinkle salad with chopped scallions. Chill until serving time. One may put a salad dressing on salad, if desired. I recommend a light mustard or poppy seed dressing.

Serves 4 to 6   Tricia Wibby

Salad Dressing

My kids say this is the best!

⅓ cup balsamic vinegar
1   tablespoon Dijon mustard
1   clove garlic, minced
⅔ cup olive oil
    Freshly ground black pepper

Put all ingredients in jar and shake vigorously. Pour on salad of any kind. Keep in refrigerator.

Serves 4 to 6   Candy Walton

Crushed garlic is more pungent than chopped.

Vance's Fancy Salad Dressing

Makes a large quantity. Popular with men.

½ onion, sliced
1   cup catsup
1   cup oil
⅔ cup sugar
1   cup vinegar
1   teaspoon salt
3   cloves garlic, pressed

In food processor mince onion and garlic. Add remaining ingredients and place in covered jar in refrigerator until ready to serve.

Vance Richardson

Tahini Dressing

½ cup olive oil
½ cup water
½ cup tahini
2   tablespoons soy sauce or tamari
2   tablespoons red wine vinegar
2   tablespoons lemon juice
    Black pepper
    Chopped fresh ginger, to taste

Combine the above and shake well. Store in refrigerator and add a little water as it thickens over time.

Marian Baker Wriggins

Watercress Salad Dressing

Buttermilk cuts the fat in half. This dressing is good on mixed greens and tomato/cucumber slices.

1   bunch watercress
1   cup buttermilk
1   scallion
1   cup real mayonnaise
    Salt and pepper to taste

In food processor or blender, purée the watercress, scallion and buttermilk. Pour into a large jar. Add the mayonnaise and lightly whisk until smooth. Add salt and pepper to taste. DO NOT put mayonnaise in processor or blender, it will liquefy.

Serves 12

Curried Salad Dressing

Goes especially well with a fruit salad.

½   cup salad oil
⅓   cup wine vinegar
1   clove garlic, minced
2   tablespoons brown sugar
2   tablespoons minced chives
1   tablespoon curry powder
1   teaspoon soy sauce

In screw top jar, combine oil, vinegar, garlic, brown sugar, chives, curry powder and soy sauce. Shake. Pour dressing over salad, tossing lightly to coat. Pass remaining dressing.

Serves 8   Marguerite Rafter

Bacon and Mustard Vinaigrette

Keeps for two weeks in refrigerator. Perfect dressing for spinach salad.

1	large egg
¼	cup tarragon or white wine vinegar
2	teaspoons Dijon mustard
2	garlic cloves, peeled
1	teaspoon salt
	White pepper to taste
¾	cup olive or sunflower oil
2	slices crumbled crisp bacon

In food processor combine egg, vinegar, mustard, garlic, salt and pepper. Whirl on and off 30 seconds. Slowly, with motor running, add oil. Then drop in bacon and process just until bits remain.

Serves 12

Sarah Marshall

Mustard Vinaigrette

This delicious salad dressing stays in solution once mixed. It goes well on any kind of greens.

2	to 3 tablespoons Dijon mustard
½	cup white wine vinegar
1	teaspoon honey
½	cup olive oil

Blend first three ingredients in a blender. While blender is still on, drizzle in oil until all is mixed. May also be mixed in a bowl in the same order. Makes approximately 1 cup.

Serves 6

Cal Harder

Vegetables, Rice and Pasta

Stairway and upper gallery of House

Spinach

This pie may be cut into small pieces for hors d'oeuvres or larger pieces for lunch (with a salad).

2   packages spinach, thawed and
    well drained
½   cup cottage cheese
1   or 2 eggs
    Muenster cheese, sliced, enough
    to line pan

Preheat oven to 350 degrees

Line pie pan with Muenster cheese. Mix spinach, cottage cheese and eggs. Place spinach mixture over cheese and bake at 350 degrees for 30 minutes or until brown on top. Cut as desired.

Lisa Witte

Spinach Artichoke Casserole

Great! Easy to make the day before.

2   cans artichoke hearts, cut into
    pieces
3   packages frozen spinach,
    defrosted and well drained
2   tablespoons sour cream
1   8-ounce package cream cheese at
    room temperature
1   cup Cheddar cheese, grated

Preheat oven to 350 degrees

Place artichoke heart pieces in greased casserole. Add spinach and salt and pepper to taste. Stir together sour cream and cream cheese and pour mixture over spinach and sprinkle top with Cheddar cheese. Bake at 350 degrees for 30 minutes.

Serves 8   Romaine S. Moloney

Stuffed Artichokes

This recipe has been enjoyed in my family for many generations. It may be served nicely with pasta or meat dishes, before or during the main course. Enjoy!

6   artichokes
1½ cups fresh bread crumbs (grated stale or toasted bread)
½   cup Parmesan cheese
    Olive oil
12 cloves garlic
    Salt
    Pepper
    Oregano
    Parsley

Select large, firm artichokes. Cut stem flush with bottom and cut top end of leaves back far enough to remove spines. For each artichoke, slice two cloves of garlic lengthwise into eight or ten pieces and push these slices down between leaves randomly so that they are held apart. Then season bread crumbs with salt, pepper, oregano and parsley, and combine with Parmesan cheese. Try to stuff all the spaces between the leaves. Top each artichoke with 2 tablespoons of olive oil. Fit them into a large pot and add about ½" of water. Cook over low to medium heat for about an hour, adding water if needed. When leaves pull out easily, artichokes are done. Let them cool in the pot and then reheat before serving. The cooling sets the seasoning.

Serves 6

Bob Cariddi
Woodworker who made the portico
and railings on McLellan-Sweat House

Spinach Ricotta Pie

Wonderful for brunch or lunch.

1   pound ricotta cheese (may use low fat ricotta)
2   packages chopped spinach, defrosted and well drained

½ pound mozzarella cheese, grated
4 eggs, slightly beaten
1 cup fresh Parmesan cheese, grated
¼ cup minced parsley
White pepper
Dash of Tabasco (optional)
1 clove of garlic, minced
1 undercooked pie crust

Preheat oven to 350 degrees

Mix all ingredients and pour into pie crust. Bake at 350 degrees approximately 1 hour until golden brown or until knife inserted in center comes out clean.

Serves 6 to 8   Beverly Kirn

Fish House Tomatoes

An easy dish that adds color to any meal.

4 ripe tomatoes
8 teaspoons minced onion
8 teaspoons brown sugar
4 teaspoons butter or margarine

Preheat oven to 350 degrees

Cut tomatoes in half and place cut side up in pan. Put 1 teaspoon minced onion on each half, followed by 1 teaspoon brown sugar and ½ teaspoon butter or margarine. Bake uncovered at 350 degrees for 45 minutes.

Serves 4   Dinny Truesdale

Fried Green Tomatoes (!!)

Great for using all those tomatoes that didn't ripen before the first frost!

4	medium-sized green tomatoes
1	tablespoon dry mustard
½	teaspoon Worcestershire sauce
2	teaspoons brown sugar
½	teaspoon salt
¼	teaspoon paprika
	Few grains cayenne pepper
	Cornmeal (or flour)
	Vegetable oil for frying

Chill tomatoes and cut in thick slices (do not peel). Mix mustard and all seasonings together. Rub in well on both sides of tomato slices. Roll slices in cornmeal and fry until brown.

Serves 6   Anne Hilliard

Tomato Spinach Casserole

Colorful and zesty with fish, lamb or broiled chicken. May be doubled.

4	boxes frozen chopped spinach
2	tablespoons lemon juice
½	cup sour cream
1	cup fresh mushrooms, sliced (or 1 8-ounce can, drained)
2	tablespoons butter or margarine
5	ripe tomatoes, sliced into ¼" pieces
	Salt and pepper to taste
1	cup grated Parmesan cheese

Preheat oven to 375 degrees

Thaw and drain spinach. Press until excess moisture is removed. Place in bowl. Add lemon juice and sour cream. Mix. Brown mushrooms in butter over medium heat. Add to spinach. Place mixture in a 2 quart casserole or soufflé dish. Place sliced tomatoes over spinach, about 3 layers. Sprinkle salt and pepper over all. Sprinkle Parmesan cheese over all. Dot with additional butter. Bake at 375 degrees for about 35 minutes or until bubbly and lightly browned.

Serves 6 to 8

Scalloped Tomatoes and Zucchini

When your late garden is overrun with tomatoes and zucchini, this casserole is a way to use these vegetables.

3	cups chopped fresh tomatoes
3	cups sliced fresh zucchini
1	medium onion, chopped
¾	cup bread crumbs
1	clove garlic, minced
1	cup sliced fresh mushrooms
1	cup grated sharp Cheddar cheese
¾	teaspoon salt
1½	teaspoons freshly ground pepper
3	tablespoons butter

Preheat oven to 350 degrees

Butter a 2-quart casserole dish. Arrange ½ of the tomatoes evenly in bottom of dish. Follow with ½ of zucchini slices. Toss together bread crumbs, onion, garlic, grated cheese, salt and pepper. Sprinkle half of this mixture over zucchini. Add ½ cup mushrooms. Repeat the process. Dot the butter over top of last layer of mushrooms. Bake 40 minutes at 350 degrees.

Serves 6 to 8   Cassie Simonds

Some Tomatoes!

Tomatoes:
- 4 cups sliced fresh tomatoes
- ½ cup chopped onion
- ¼ cup all purpose flour
- 2 to 6 tablespoons brown sugar
- 1 teaspoon baking powder
- 1 teaspoon chopped fresh oregano
- ½ teaspoon salt
- ⅓ cup water
- 1 egg, beaten
- 1 tablespoon lemon juice

Topping:
- ¾ cup all purpose flour
- 1 teaspoon grated lemon peel
- ½ teaspoon salt
- ¼ teaspoon pepper
- 2 to 5 tablespoons sugar
- 1 teaspoon ground cumin
- ½ cup butter, softened

Preheat oven to 375 degrees

Tomatoes: arrange tomato slices in greased 2 quart shallow casserole or 12" x 8" baking dish. Sprinkle with chopped onion. In mixing bowl, combine flour, brown sugar, baking powder, oregano, salt, water, egg and lemon juice. Beat with rotary beater just until smooth. Pour over tomatoes and onion. Cover casserole with aluminum foil. Bake at 375 degrees for 20 minutes. Remove from oven.

Topping: combine flour, lemon peel, salt, pepper and sugar. Cut in butter until mixture resembles coarse crumbs. Sprinkle topping over tomatoes. Return to oven uncovered and bake for 20 to 25 minutes longer until topping is crisp and light brown.

Serves 6 to 8

Mrs. Widgery Thomas, Jr.

Asparagus Roulades

16 spears fresh asparagus
8   slices ham
1   cup sour cream
2   tablespoons stone-ground
    mustard
8   ounces grated Cheddar cheese
    Garnish of fresh chives

Steam asparagus al dente. Roll 2 spears in one piece of ham. Place in a 9" x 13" pan. Combine sour cream and mustard, mixing well. Spoon over asparagus rolls. Sprinkle cheese on top. Broil until cheese melts and rolls are warm.

Serves 8   Beverly Kirn

Sesame Broccoli

1   tablespoon soy sauce
1   tablespoon sesame oil
¼   cup vermouth
2   teaspoons honey
2   heads broccoli, cut into flowerets
1   tablespoon sesame seeds, toasted

Combine soy sauce, sesame oil, vermouth and honey. Set aside. Steam broccoli until tender but still crisp. Drain. Toss broccoli and dressing together. Sprinkle with sesame seeds and serve.

Serves 8

*Salt in the water keeps
green beans from fading.*

Green Bean Casserole

This goes well with any seafood, rice dish or salad.

½ cup sliced onion
1 tablespoon minced parsley
2 tablespoons butter
2 tablespoons flour
1 teaspoon salt
¼ teaspoon pepper
Grated rind of ½ lemon
1 cup sour cream
5 cups cooked French-style string beans
½ cup grated mild Cheddar cheese
½ cup bread crumbs
2 tablespoons butter, melted

Preheat oven to 325 degrees

Sauté first seven ingredients until golden brown. Add sour cream and mix. Stir in green beans. Pour into baking dish. Combine cheese and bread crumbs which have been mixed with melted butter. Add to top of casserole. Bake at 325 degrees until hot and cheese melts, about 30 minutes.

Serves 6 to 8   Norm Marshall

Parmesan Eggplant Gratiné

Delicious with beef and chicken. It is a nice replacement for potato, rice or pasta.

1 medium sized eggplant
4 tablespoons butter
4 tablespoons grated Parmesan cheese
Parmesan cheese for sprinkling

Preheat oven to 425 degrees

Wash eggplant, leaving skin on. Slice in ½" slices. Place on large bread board and salt. Leave standing for ½ hour. The salt will take the bitterness out of the raw eggplant. In a small bowl, place 4 tablespoons of soft butter and add 4 tablespoons Parmesan cheese. Stir and mix. Butter both sides of eggplant generously. Sprinkle Parmesan on top. Place on cookie sheet. Bake in 425 degree oven for 10 minutes. Broil for about 5 minutes until browned.

Serves 3 to 4   Janneke S. J. Neilson
                                                                              Trustee

Green Beans with Basil

3	tablespoons butter
½	cup chopped onion
¼	cup chopped celery
1	clove garlic, minced
½	teaspoon dried rosemary
½	teaspoon dried basil (if fresh, use 2 teaspoons)
1	pound green beans

Melt butter. Add all remaining ingredients except beans and cook until onions and celery are clear. Cook beans in separate pan until crunchy. Drain. Toss in the basil sauce and serve.

Serves 5 to 6   Mary Haggerty
                          Lincoln House Country Inn, Dennysville

*To add flavor to frozen peas,
add fresh mint when cooking.*

Grilled Vegetables

1 medium eggplant
2 zucchini
4 plum tomatoes
  Soy sauce
  Olive oil
  Black/Szechuan pepper mix

Cut eggplant in ½" slices, leave skin on. Cut zucchini in half, lengthwise. Cut tomatoes in half, lengthwise. Brush cut vegetables lightly with soy sauce, then with olive oil. Dust with ground pepper mix. Grill over hot coals. Turn zucchini and eggplant once.

Leslie Otten
President of the Board of Trustees

Vegetarian Chili

Wonderful for large crowds of young people. Serve with rice and salad. May be halved or doubled easily.

2 tablespoons olive or cooking oil
1½ cups chopped celery
1½ cups chopped green pepper
1 cup chopped onion
3 cloves garlic, minced
2 28-ounce cans tomatoes, cut up
3 16-ounce cans red kidney beans, rinsed and drained
½ cup raisins
½ cup red wine vinegar
1 tablespoon chili powder
1 tablespoon snipped parsley
2 teaspoons salt
1½ teaspoons dried oregano, crushed
1½ teaspoons dried basil, crushed
1½ teaspoons ground cumin
1 teaspoon ground allspice
¼ teaspoon pepper

¼ teaspoon bottled hot pepper
sauce
1 bay leaf
1 12-ounce can (1½ cups) beer
¾ cup cashew nuts
1 cup shredded Swiss, mozzarella
or Cheddar cheese

Heat oil in 4½ quart Dutch oven (I use a large chowder pot). Add celery, green pepper, onion and garlic. Cook covered until vegetables are tender but not brown. Stir in undrained tomatoes, drained beans, raisins, vinegar, chili powder, parsley, salt, basil, oregano, cumin, allspice, pepper, pepper sauce and bay leaf. Bring to boil, reduce heat and simmer, covered, for 1½ hours. Stir in beer and cashews. Return to boil, then simmer, uncovered, 30 minutes more or until desired consistency. Remove bay leaf. Sprinkle cheese atop each serving.

Serves 6 to 8   Jane Smith Moody

Spiced Beets

Delicious hot as vegetable or cold in salad.

2   bunches medium sized beets, to
make 1 to 1½ pints when cooked
⅛ cup vinegar
¾ cup sugar
½ cup water
1 teaspoon ground cinnamon
¼ teaspoon ground allspice
¼ teaspoon ground cloves
½ teaspoon salt
2 teaspoons lemon juice

Cook beets in salted water until done. Remove skins and slice (should be about 1 to 1½ pints of sliced beets). To make dressing, mix remaining ingredients together and bring to a boil. Add sliced beets and simmer 8 minutes.

Serves 6 to 8   Mrs. Horace W. Peters

Chili Rellenos Casserole

This goes well with margaritas and art from Santa Fe!

1	can green chili peppers (Ortega 16-ounce or 4 small 4-ounce cans)
1	pound Cheddar cheese, grated
1	pound Monterey Jack cheese, grated
4	eggs, separated
1	can evaporated milk
2	tablespoons flour
½	teaspoon salt
¼	teaspoon black pepper
1	8-ounce can tomato sauce

Preheat oven to 350 degrees

Wash and seed green chili peppers. Cut open and place one layer of peppers in a 9" x 13" casserole dish. Add grated Cheddar cheese over the peppers. Place another layer of peppers over this. Add the grated Jack cheese. Beat yolks and combine with evaporated milk. Add flour, salt and pepper to egg mixture. Beat whites until stiff. Fold in. Pour this combined mixture on top of peppers and cheeses (do not mix). Bake at 350 degrees for 45 minutes. Remove and pour on top the tomato sauce (do not mix). Return to oven and continue to bake until tomato sauce crusts at the edge of the dish.

Serves 8

John Upton
Trustee

Easy Corn Fritters

Delicious for light lunch.

6	ears of fresh corn, cut from cob
2	eggs, separated
½	teaspoon salt
3	tablespoons milk

2　tablespoons flour
Oil for greasing

Cut corn from cob. Beat 2 yolks until light yellow. Add to corn with salt, milk and flour. Beat 2 whites until they hold their shape and then fold into corn mixture. Put large spoonfuls in hot greased frying pan or on griddle and cook until golden brown. Turn and repeat. Serve with syrup, jelly or just butter.

Serves 4   Libby Porter

Maine Grandmother's Corn Fritters

When Grandmother was visiting us she would make doughnuts and apple or corn fritters. It was wonderful to come home to lunch after a morning at school and see her frying those golden corn puffs. They may be served with honey but I think maple syrup is best.

½　cup unsifted flour
½　teaspoon baking powder
¼　teaspoon salt
1　egg, separated
3　tablespoons milk
1　quart corn oil (divided)
1　cup whole kernel corn (canned, frozen and thawed, or fresh)

In medium bowl, stir together flour, baking powder and salt. Beat egg yolk slightly. Stir in milk and 1 teaspoon of the corn oil. Add to flour mixture. Stir just until mixed. Stir in corn. In small bowl with mixer at high speed, beat egg white until stiff peaks form. Fold into corn mixture. Pour remaining corn oil into deep skillet, filling no more than ⅓ full. Heat over medium heat to 375 degrees using a frying thermometer. Carefully add batter by tablespoons, a few at a time. Fry, turning once, 3 to 4 minutes, or until golden brown. Drain on paper towels.

For apple fritters: in place of corn, use 1 cup chopped, peeled apple. If desired, sprinkle with confectioners' sugar before serving.

Serves 6 to 8   Beatrice H. Comas

Potato Puff

8   potatoes, peeled
¼   to ½ cup milk
2   eggs, separated
1   cup cottage cheese
½   cup sour cream
1   tablespoon grated onion
2   teaspoons salt
2   teaspoons dill weed
    Paprika
    Pepper
    Parsley, chopped
    Grated Cheddar cheese
    Milk

Preheat oven to 350 degrees

Cut potatoes into 2 inch square pieces. Boil in salted water for 20 minutes or until done. Drain. Mash potatoes with milk (should be fairly stiff). Add beaten egg yolks, cottage cheese, sour cream, salt, pepper to taste, dill and grated onion. Beat egg whites until stiff but not dry. Fold into potato mixture. Pour into buttered 2 quart casserole. Top with parsley, cheese, and sprinkle paprika over all. Bake at 350 degrees for 45 minutes.

Serves 8 to 10   Lisa Toner

Rosemary Potatoes

Rave reviews. Great with beef, lamb and fish.

2   dozen small new potatoes
4   large garlic cloves, chopped
3   tablespoons fresh rosemary, chopped
¼   cup olive oil
    Salt and pepper to taste

Preheat oven to 400 degrees

Wash potatoes. Steam for 8 minutes or until just done. Chop fresh garlic and set aside. Snip and chop rosemary, and set aside. Pour olive oil into a pan. Put into oven for about five minutes. Carefully place garlic in and cook for a few minutes (to brown slightly). Cut potatoes into halves or quarters, depending on size. Carefully place them into pan. Add rosemary, salt and pepper. Stir so potatoes are coated with oil. Bake for approximately 45 minutes, uncovered, until brown and crusty. Stir occasionally during cooking.

Serves 8   Margaret Wilkis

North Shore Potatoes

6	medium potatoes, boiled
2	cups sour cream
½	medium onion, chopped
6	tablespoons butter
2	cups Cheddar cheese, cut into pieces
½	teaspoon salt
½	teaspoon pepper

Preheat oven to 350 degrees

Boil and store potatoes in refrigerator until cool enough to peel. Melt butter and cheese together. Add sour cream, salt, pepper and onion. Stir until blended. Peel and grate potatoes, add to other ingredients and put in casserole. Bake at 350 degrees for 45 minutes.

Serves 6   Rachel F. Armstrong
                                        Chairman of the Board of Trustees

Diced or julienned potatoes, cooked in half & half (or whole milk) in top of double boiler (no water) until done, are easy and sensational. Best made a day or two ahead, placed in baking dish and reheated before serving.

Sweet Potato-Carrot Purée

Wonderful make-ahead dish. Excellent served with lamb, pork or chicken and a green vegetable.

2   large sweet potatoes, baked
1   small package carrots (approximately 6-8 carrots), cooked
1   to 3 tablespoons butter or margarine, as desired
¼ cup light cream or milk
    Salt and freshly ground pepper, to taste
    Dash of nutmeg

Preheat oven to 325 degrees

Mix all ingredients in food processor and place in shallow buttered baking dish. May be made a day or two ahead and kept refrigerated. Remove from refrigerator and bring to room temperature. Bake at 325 degrees for 30 to 40 minutes.

Serves 4 to 6

Tinker Barron

Potatoes on the Grill

4   potatoes (8 ounces each), thinly sliced ⅛" thick
1   to 2 onions (8 ounces each), sliced in rings
    Butter
    Salt and pepper
    Sprinkle of fresh dill weed

Wash potatoes and slice. Do not peel them. Place potatoes on a sheet of heavy aluminum foil. Top with onions. Sprinkle with salt and pepper and fresh dill weed. Dot with plenty of butter. Seal foil securely, forming a packet. Cook on charcoal or gas grill at medium heat, turning once, about 20-30 minutes each side.

Serves 4

Nonie Pierce

Buttered Oven Potatoes

4 medium baking potatoes, peeled
and sliced
½ stick melted butter
Ice water
Salt and ground black pepper
Dill weed or parsley

Preheat oven to 375 degrees

Slice potatoes into lengths (like French fries). Soak for 1 hour in ice water. Remove and dry on paper towel. Dip each piece of potato into the melted butter. Arrange in a shallow baking pan. Season to taste with salt and pepper. Bake at 375 degrees until potatoes are brown and tender. Sprinkle with dill or parsley.

Serves 6   Cassie Simonds

Yams Cointreau

Good, easy.

4 large yams or sweet potatoes,
about 3½ pounds
¼ cup Cointreau
¼ cup butter, melted
1 teaspoon salt
Dash of pepper
Parsley for garnish, chopped

Cook yams in boiling water to cover for 30 minutes or until tender. Drain, cool and peel. Mash yams. Stir in next 4 ingredients. Garnish with chopped parsley and serve.

Serves 6 to 8   Prudence D. Gilmore

Baked Beans

2 16-ounce cans small baked beans
6 tablespoons catsup
1 tablespoon Worcestershire sauce
3 tablespoons dark brown sugar, packed
1 teaspoon dry mustard
3 tablespoons grated onion

Preheat oven to 325 degrees

Bake partially covered in a 2½ quart casserole at 325 degrees for 1½ hours. Serve.

Serves 6 to 8   Barbara Bush

Rice with Summer Vegetables

Very good with grilled meat, fish or chicken. Any leftovers are delicious cold.

1 cup long-grain white rice
2 small summer squash or zucchini, sliced
1 medium onion, coarsely chopped
1 cup sliced mushrooms
2 cups fresh green beans (cut) or 1 package frozen
¼ cup chopped fresh basil (or 2 teaspoons dried)
2 medium tomatoes, seeded and coarsely chopped
1½ cups V-8 juice
1 teaspoon salt
½ teaspoon pepper
  Few drops Tabasco
2 teaspoons brown sugar
4 tablespoons butter

Preheat oven to 350 degrees

Butter casserole and add ½ cup rice, ½ of vegetables and ½ of seasonings. Dot with half of butter. Repeat layering with remaining ingredients. Add V-8 juice and bake at 350 degrees, covered, for ¾ to 1 hour or until vegetables and rice are tender. Add more liquid if necessary.

Serves 8   Wilma P. Redman

Quarters #8 Parsley Rice Soufflé

2 cups cooked rice
2 cups grated sharp cheese
2 tablespoons melted butter
1 cup milk
1 tablespoon salt
1 large onion, finely chopped
¾ cup chopped parsley
1 tablespoon Worcestershire sauce
2 eggs, separated

Preheat oven to 350 degrees

Combine rice, cheese, butter and other ingredients, except eggs. Beat egg yolks and whites separately. Fold into rice ingredients. Pour into a well buttered casserole. Bake at 350 degrees for 1 hour or until set and lightly browned.

Serves 4

To "dress up" white or brown rice, mix ½ teaspoon
finely grated orange (or lemon) rind and chopped parsley.

Green and Yellow Rice

I've cooked for family and friends from Dover-Foxcroft, Maine to Los Angeles, California. Everyone, even those who "hate" spinach, loves my Green and Yellow Rice!

3	cups cooked rice
¼	cup butter or margarine
4	eggs
1	cup milk
1	pound sharp yellow Cheddar cheese, grated
1	package frozen chopped spinach, cooked and well drained
1	small onion, minced
1	tablespoon Worcestershire sauce
½	teaspoon each: marjoram, thyme, rosemary and salt

Preheat oven to 350 degrees

Melt butter and add to rice. Beat eggs in a large bowl. Add milk and then cheese. Add spinach, onion, Worcestershire sauce and seasonings. Mix well, but gently. Stir in rice. Place in a 3 quart casserole dish (may be covered and refrigerated until ready to bake). Set, uncovered, in a shallow pan of warm water and bake at 350 degrees for 45 minutes or until piping hot.

Serves 8   Jan Nelligan

Green Rice Ring

Ring may be filled with seafood or vegetables for an easy supper served with salad and fruit.

2	cups cooked rice
1	bunch scallions, finely chopped
½	cup finely chopped parsley
½	cup finely chopped celery
3	eggs, separated
½	cup heavy cream

½ cup butter
Salt
Pepper
Dry bread crumbs

Preheat oven to 450 degrees

Combine all ingredients except egg whites. Beat whites until stiff. Fold into rice mixture. Butter ring mold. Generously line with cracker crumbs. Pour rice mixture into mold. Place mold in pan of water. Bake at 450 degrees for 45 minutes or until set. When set, turn out onto round platter. Prepare ahead except for eggs.

Serves 4 to 6   D. Lombard Brett

Wild Rice (In the Oven)

Easy and delicious!

2   cups wild rice
¼   pound butter
4¼ cups of chicken broth

Preheat oven to 325 degrees

Wash wild rice thoroughly. Melt butter in frying pan. Add rice and cook for five minutes. Remove rice to casserole (with cover). Add 4¼ cups chicken broth. Stir well. Cook covered at 325 degrees for 1¼ hours. Stir occasionally.

Serves 6 to 8   Lisa Witte

Try cooking rice in a double boiler; it's great!

Baked Noodles

Excellent with roast veal. For a party, add 1 cup chopped ham and/or 1 cup mushrooms, sliced and sautéed in butter.

1   6-ounce package fine noodles
1   cup cottage cheese with chives
1   cup sour cream
1   clove garlic, minced
1   small to medium onion, finely chopped
1   tablespoon Worcestershire sauce
   Dash of Tabasco sauce
   Salt

Preheat oven to 350 degrees

Cook noodles in three quarts of boiling salted water, uncovered, for three minutes. Drain. Mix other ingredients and add to noodles. Put in buttered casserole dish. Bake at 350 degrees for 45 minutes or until brown and crunchy on top.

Serves 4 to 6   Nonie Pierce

Noodles Waterfold

May be prepared ahead.

1   box or package no-yolk egg noodles
1   pound creamed cottage cheese
3   cups sour cream
1   medium onion, minced (Vidalia, when in season)
1   clove garlic, minced
1   tablespoon Worcestershire sauce
1   teaspoon fresh ground black pepper
¼   pound lightly salted butter and for dotting

1   teaspoon salt
    Pepper
    Parmesan cheese for topping

Preheat oven to 350 degrees

Cook noodles 10 minutes or until tender. Drain and place in buttered casserole. Melt butter in skillet. Sauté garlic and onion until transparent. Blend and heat remaining ingredients. Combine with noodles. Sprinkle with Parmesan cheese. Dot with butter. Cover with foil. Bake at 350 degrees for 45 minutes. Uncover and bake 15 minutes. Serve with extra cheese and sour cream.

Serves 6 to 8

Fettuccine with Cherry Tomatoes, Goat Cheese, and Herbs

May be doubled easily.

½   pound fettuccine
¼   cup vegetable oil
1   tablespoon minced garlic
3   tablespoons minced fresh parsley
    leaves, or to taste
2   tablespoons minced fresh mint
    leaves
1½ cups cherry tomatoes, quartered
3   ounces mild goat cheese,
    crumbled (about ¾ cup)

In a kettle of boiling salted water cook the fettuccine until it is al dente. When the fettuccine is cooking, in a small saucepan heat the oil and the garlic over moderately low heat just until the mixture is hot. Remove the pan from the heat. Drain the fettuccine well and in a bowl toss it with the oil and garlic, minced parsley, mint, tomatoes, goat cheese, and salt and pepper to taste. Serve immediately.

Serves 2 to 4   Mead Brownell

Lasagna with Cilantro

1	large can whole tomatoes
1	regular can tomato sauce
1	small can tomato paste
3	tablespoons olive oil
1	onion, chopped
1	pound mushrooms, chopped
2	or 3 garlic cloves, chopped
3	eggs, beaten
2	pounds ricotta or cottage cheese
¼	cup Parmesan cheese
1	package thawed chopped spinach, well drained Bunch of fresh cilantro, chopped oregano, basil, salt, pepper (all to taste) Bay leaf
1	cup red wine Few squirts Worcestershire sauce
2	12-ounce packages grated mozzarella
9	to 12 pieces lasagna noodles

Preheat oven to 350 degrees

Sauté mushrooms, onions and garlic in olive oil. Split this mixture in half and set aside. Add to the remaining (in big skillet) the tomato sauce, paste and tomatoes. Add also the oregano, basil, salt, pepper (all to taste), bay leaf, red wine, Worcestershire and fresh cilantro. Let simmer 15 to 20 minutes. During this time, cook the lasagna noodles. In a bowl, combine beaten eggs, ricotta or cottage cheese, the rest of the sautéed mushrooms, onion and garlic mixture, ¼ cup Parmesan and thawed spinach. Layer in a greased lasagna pan in the following order: pasta, ricotta mixture, mozzarella, and sauce (I can usually do 3 layers in this order; try to end with sauce). Cover with foil. Bake at 350 degrees for 40 minutes. Remove foil, bake another 10-15 minutes.

Marian Baker Wriggins

Ziti with Asparagus and Mushrooms

3   tablespoons vegetable oil
1   pound asparagus cut into 1½"
    pieces, tough ends removed
    Salt and pepper to taste
2   tablespoons chopped fresh basil
    or 1 tablespoon dried
2   cups sliced mushrooms (not too
    thin)
4   cups chopped canned tomatoes,
    drained
1   pound ziti or other tubular pasta
    Parsley, chopped, for garnish

Heat the oil in a skillet and sauté the asparagus. Add salt and pepper and cook over medium heat, stirring often, about 5 minutes. Do not overcook. Remove with a slotted spoon and set aside. Add the mushrooms to the oil, salt and pepper again to taste, and sauté over high heat. When mushrooms begin to brown, add tomatoes and basil. Simmer in sauce 5 minutes; then add asparagus and simmer another 5 minutes. Meanwhile, cook the pasta until just done. Drain well and mix with the sauce. Garnish with parsley and serve.

Serves 6 to 8

*Dried herbs should be replaced
every year. They have lost their flavor by then.*

Pasta with Green Tomatoes I

What a great way for all the green tomatoes in the fall.

5   tablespoons vegetable oil
2   medium onions, finely chopped
1   teaspoon finely chopped garlic
4   large green tomatoes, thinly
    sliced (about 8 cups)
2   tablespoons finely chopped
    parsley
3   tablespoons coarsely chopped
    fresh basil
½   to 1 cup chicken stock
    Salt and freshly ground black
    pepper to taste
1   pound rigatoni or tubular pasta
7   tablespoons freshly grated
    Parmesan cheese
    Parsley

Heat the oil in a medium saucepan or skillet. Add onion and simmer over moderate heat until it begins to brown. Add garlic, simmer a minute or so, then add tomatoes. Cover and simmer over medium to low heat for 5 minutes. Add parsley, basil, ½ cup stock, salt and pepper. Cover and simmer over medium heat, adding more stock if sauce becomes too dry. Cook for 30 minutes. When tomatoes are nearly done, cook pasta. Drain well and toss with sauce. Add cheese, mix, and serve immediately. Garnish with chopped parsley.

Serves 6 to 8

Breads and Spreads

Fence detail beneath Copper Beech Tree

Lincoln Park Spoon Bread

Excellent with steak and kidney pie.

¾ cup cornmeal
2 cups milk
½ teaspoon salt
1 tablespoon butter
4 eggs, separated
1 tablespoon baking powder

Preheat oven to 400 degrees

Let milk come to a boil and slowly add cornmeal, salt and butter. Simmer until thickened. Stir in slightly beaten egg yolks while cooking. Then fold in beaten whites. Pour into greased soufflé-type dish. Place in pan of water and bake in 400 degree oven for 45 minutes.

Debbie Farnsworth Knecht

Lemon Tea Bread

6 tablespoons butter or margarine
1 cup sugar
2 eggs
1½ cups sifted flour
1 teaspoon baking powder
½ cup milk
¼ teaspoon salt
½ cup nut meats
Grated rind of one lemon

Preheat oven to 350 degrees

Cream shortening and sugar with grated lemon rind. Add eggs. Beat. Blend in flour, baking powder and salt. Pour into greased loaf pan. Bake for 1 hour in 350 degree oven or until toothpick comes out clean. Mix ¼ cup sugar and juice of one lemon. Pour over top of bread while hot. Let cool in pan.

Makes one loaf   Marilyn Spencer

Persimmon Nut Bread

Excellent served warm or cold. Warm brings out the flavor. Good with cream cheese.

2	cups flour
1	teaspoon baking powder
½	teaspoon salt
1	cup sugar
6	ounces butter
2	eggs, well beaten
1	cup persimmon pulp
1	cup chopped pecans

Preheat oven to 325 degrees

Wash the persimmons, peel and mash, reserving seedless pulp. Sift together the flour, baking powder and salt. Set aside. Cream the butter and sugar. Add the eggs, persimmon pulp and the chopped nuts. Mix and pour into the flour mixture and mix again. Pour into two small greased and floured loaf pans or one large one. Bake one hour at 325 degrees or until toothpick comes out clean.

Mrs. John McInnes III

Banana Nut Bread

Easy preparation! Good results every time!

2	to 3 ripe bananas
1½	cups sifted flour
½	cup melted margarine or butter
1	cup sugar
1	teaspoon vanilla
1	egg, beaten
¼	teaspoon salt
1	teaspoon baking soda
1	cup chopped nuts (optional)

Preheat oven to 350 degrees

Mash bananas. Blend in sugar, egg and melted butter. Sift flour and dry ingredients. Mix together until well blended. Add nuts. Pour into greased loaf pan. Sprinkle top with sugar and bake in oven 50 minutes at 350 degrees or until toothpick comes out clean. Cool on rack before removing from pan. Serve at room temperature. May be wrapped in foil and frozen.

Marjorie S. Soden

Blueberry Bread

It is even better on 2nd day, toasted.

1 egg, beaten
½ cup sugar
1 cup flour
1 teaspoon baking powder
  Salt
½ cup milk
1 tablespoon melted butter, margarine or salad oil
1 cup blueberries

Preheat oven to 400 degrees

Beat egg. Beat in the sugar, flour, baking powder, salt, milk and shortening, to blend. Gently stir in the blueberries. Spread mixture on greased jelly roll pan. It will be thin. Bake at 400 degrees for 15 minutes. Briefly brown top under broiler. Serve with butter or margarine.

Serves 6

Anne Woodbury
Robert Woodbury, Chancellor
University of Maine

*To reduce cholesterol, substitute
¼ cup Egg Beater for each egg.*

Onion, Cheese, and Walnut Muffins

1¾ cups flour
¼ cup sugar
2 teaspoons baking powder
1 beaten egg
¾ cup milk
⅓ cup cooking oil
1 onion, coarsely chopped
½ cup shredded Cheddar cheese
½ cup chopped walnuts

Preheat oven to 400 degrees

In a large mixing bowl stir together the flour, sugar and baking powder. Make a well in the center. Combine egg, milk and oil. Add egg mixture all at once to flour mixture, stir just until moistened. Stir in onion, cheese and walnuts. Grease or line muffin cups and fill approximately ⅔ full. Bake at 400 degrees for 20 to 25 minutes or until golden.

Makes 12 muffins   Karin Lundgren

Poppy Seed and Orange Muffins

¾ cup sugar
¼ cup softened butter
1½ teaspoons grated orange peel, fresh or dried
2 eggs
2 cups flour
2½ teaspoons baking powder
½ teaspoon salt
¼ teaspoon ground nutmeg
1 cup milk
½ cup raisins
½ cup walnuts
5 tablespoons poppy seeds

Preheat oven to 400 degrees

Cream sugar, butter and orange peel. Add eggs and mix well. Combine flour, baking powder, salt and nutmeg. Add to creamed mixture alternately with milk, mixing lightly. Fold in raisins, nuts and poppy seeds. Spoon batter into greased muffin tins or use paper baking cups, filling to ¾ full. Bake at 400 degrees for 20 minutes or until tops are golden. Serve warm. Batter may be made in advance and stored in refrigerator for up to four days.

Makes 12 muffins   Mary Haggerty
                          Lincoln House Country Inn, Dennysville

Brown Sugar Oatmeal Muffins

A favorite of breakfast customers at Christine's Dream.

1½ cups oats
1½ cups whole wheat flour
¾   cup all purpose flour
3   teaspoons baking powder
¾   teaspoon salt
3   eggs
1   cup and 2 tablespoons brown
      sugar
1   cup and 2 tablespoons milk
3   ounces butter, melted

Preheat oven to 375 degrees

Mix dry ingredients in bowl. Mix egg, milk and melted butter. Pour over dry ingredients and fold in gently, just until moistened. Bake in greased or paper lined muffin pans at 375 degrees for 15 to 20 minutes.

Makes 12 muffins   Christine Serrage Burke
                                Christine's Dream, Portland

Blueberry Muffins

6   tablespoons butter
1½ cups sugar
2   large eggs
2   cups flour
½   teaspoon salt
2   teaspoons baking powder
½   cup milk
1   pint blueberries
2   teaspoons each sugar and
    cinnamon

Preheat oven to 375 degrees

Cream butter and sugar well. Add eggs and beat well. Add flour, salt and baking powder. Add milk gradually, stirring until just moistened. Crush ½ cup of blueberries with fork and mix into batter. Add remaining blueberries. Spoon into lined baking cups or greased muffin tins. Bake at 375 degrees for 30 minutes. Sprinkle top with cinnamon and sugar (mixed).

Makes 12 muffins

Louise Montgomery
Artist's Wife
Beloved community leader

Bran Muffins

It takes an hour to get the ingredients mixed but you have the "makings" of delicious bran muffins for up to 6 weeks in the refrigerator.

5   cups flour
2¾ cups sugar
1   15-ounce package raisin bran
1   cup raisins
1   cup chopped walnuts
5   teaspoons baking soda
2   teaspoons salt
1   quart buttermilk
4   eggs, lightly beaten
1   cup vegetable oil

Preheat oven to 400 degrees

Combine first 7 ingredients and blend well. Combine buttermilk, eggs and oil and stir into the dry ingredients. Put mixture in a covered container and refrigerate overnight. Fill greased muffin tins ¾ full and bake 20 minutes at 400 degrees. Refrigerate remaining ingredients for later use.

Makes 48 to 60 muffins   Maribel Lord

Jordan Pond House Popovers

One of our family's gems.

2	large eggs
1	cup whole milk
1	cup sifted all purpose flour
¼	teaspoon salt
	Speck of baking soda

Preheat oven to 425 degrees

Beat the two eggs at high speed until lemon colored. On slowest speed, add very slowly one half cup of the milk and beat until well mixed. Sift flour, salt and soda. Add slowly (with the mixer going on slow speed) the dry ingredients. When mixed, stop the beater and scrape sides of bowl with spatula, then turn to maximum speed and slowly add the rest of the milk. Beat two minutes. Turn to high speed and beat five to seven minutes. Batter should be smooth and about the thickness of heavy cream. Pour batter into well greased muffin tins or custard cups. It is not necessary to heat these before using. If a muffin tin is used, fill to the top if you wish large, high popovers. Bake on middle shelf of 425 degree oven for first 15 minutes. Without opening oven, reduce temperature to 350 degrees and bake 15 to 20 minutes longer. They are best when served at once, but may be kept in oven for an additional 4 to 5 minutes.

Barbara Y. Sturgeon

Port and Grape Jelly

A classic for the holidays for many years. Good for presents as well as for dinner! Especially fine with lamb or game.

3 cups sugar
1 box powdered pectin
½ cup bottled grape juice
1½ cups port wine
1 cup water

Measure sugar into a bowl. Mix the pectin with the juice, port and water in a 5 to 6 quart saucepan. Stir until the pectin has dissolved. Place over high heat and stir until the mixture comes to a full rolling boil. Add the sugar at once and return to hard boil. Boil one minute, stirring constantly. Remove the jelly from the heat, skim off the foam and pour at once into hot sterilized glasses. Seal with paraffin.

Sally W. Rand

Tomato Fruit Relish

Goes very well with grilled meats and hamburgers. It is worth the preparation time.

30 to 35 large peeled tomatoes
6 green peppers, seeded and chopped (or 3 red and 3 green peppers may be used)
6 onions, peeled and chopped
6 peaches, peeled and pitted (may be a little unripe or imperfect)
6 pears, peeled and cored (may be a little unripe or imperfect)
3 cups sugar
1 pint white vinegar
2 tablespoons salt
3 or 4 tablespoons mixed pickling spice in cheesecloth

Chop everything in a large bowl. Place chopped fruit in large pot. Add vinegar, sugar, spices and salt. Bring to a boil. Cook briskly (medium heat) for about 2 hours. Stir frequently with wooden spoon making sure fruit is not sticking to the bottom. Mixture will thicken. When it is the consistency of "applesauce," stop cooking and spoon into sterilized pint jars. Seal. Sterilize jars by placing in a pan filled with water; add water to cover jars and boil for 15 to 20 minutes. Use self-sealing lids. Enjoy!

Makes 6 to 8 pints   Linda Frinsko

Rouge

Great condiment with meats.

5	to 6 ripe tomatoes
1	onion, chopped
3	to 4 stalks celery, chopped
1	garlic clove, minced
	Pinch salt
2	tablespoons brown sugar
2	tablespoons white vinegar
⅛	teaspoon ground cloves
⅛	teaspoon ground cinnamon
	Freshly ground black pepper

Place all ingredients in saucepan. Bring to simmer over medium low heat. Turn heat to lowest setting and continue simmering, uncovered, about 1 hour. Taste and adjust seasoning. Keeps in refrigerator 1 to 2 weeks. May be frozen or canned.

Yield: approximately 1 quart   Patricia Clark

Grating rinds of lemon, lime or orange
should be done while the fruit is still whole.

Hot Spiced Fruit Compote

Serve as a meat accompaniment.

1	16-ounce can peach halves
3	4-inch cinnamon sticks
6	whole cloves
¼	teaspoon nutmeg
¼	teaspoon light brown sugar, firmly packed
1	tablespoon lemon juice
1	lime, grated zest and juice
1	large can pear halves, drained
1	large can apricot halves, drained

Drain peaches, reserving liquid. In saucepan, combine peach liquid, cinnamon sticks, cloves, nutmeg, sugar, lemon juice, lime juice and grated zest. Bring to a boil. Reduce heat and simmer, uncovered, 5 minutes. Add peaches, pears, and apricots to hot syrup. Cook over low heat 15 minutes. Cool and let stand in marinade. Refrigerate overnight. Heat and serve.

Bonnie Lee Nelson

Apricot Ginger Chutney

A wonderful accompaniment for freshly grilled fish, meat or poultry.

2	cups dried apricots
1½	tablespoons chopped candied ginger
1	cup dark raisins
½	lime, thinly sliced
1	large onion, thinly sliced
1½	cups packed dark brown sugar
½	to 1 cup orange juice
½	cup wine vinegar
3	cloves garlic, minced
1	teaspoon dried mustard
½	cup tomato sauce

½   teaspoon cinnamon
½   teaspoon allspice
½   teaspoon cloves

Wash and chop apricots. Combine all ingredients in a medium saucepan and simmer 20 minutes, stirring often until slightly thickened. Pour cool chutney into a covered container and refrigerate. May be served cold or at room temperature.

Serves 10 to 12 or more   Judy Glickman

Molded Cranberry Pineapple Conserve

Choose your most charming mold. The effect enhances the table as well as the dinner. Also try muffin tin for individual salads arranged with greens on plates or platter.

2   cups crushed pineapple
1   cup finely chopped celery
1   can cranberry sauce
1   cup chopped walnuts
1   tablespoon Knox gelatin
1   box strawberry Jello
1   cup hot water
    Pinch of salt

Pour hot water over Jello, add salt. Dissolve gelatin in ¼ cup cold water. Combine gelatin and Jello mixtures. Add cranberry sauce while mixture is warm, not hot. Add celery, walnuts and pineapple. Pour in mold and chill until set. Will keep for days in refrigerator.

Debbie Farnsworth Knecht

*Lemon zest is the colored part of the peel
excluding the white pith, which adds bitterness.*

Oignons à la Grecque or Greek Onions

Makes an excellent hors d'oeuvre and also goes well with roast meats, particularly game.

3	tablespoons butter
2	pounds small white onions
¾	cup chicken broth
¾	cup seedless raisins or dark currants
¼	cup wine vinegar
1	tablespoon salad oil
2	tablespoons sugar
3	tablespoons tomato paste
½	teaspoon salt and pepper
¼	teaspoon thyme
1	bay leaf, crumbled
½	teaspoon red pepper flakes

Preheat oven to 325 degrees

Sauté onions in large skillet in butter until well browned. Combine all other ingredients and simmer 2 or 3 minutes. Arrange in shallow baking dish or casserole and cover with sauce. Bake in 325 degree oven, uncovered, for one hour. Refrigerate. Serve chilled from casserole.

Serves 10 to 12   Alfred C. Chadbourn
                                                                    Artist

*In cooking, use only wine
that you would drink.*

Seafood:
Chowders and Entrées

L. D. M. Sweat Memorial Galleries

"Spite House" Crab or Lobster Stew

This is the most delicious soup ever!

½ cup butter
6 tablespoons flour
1½ quarts whole milk
1 pint heavy cream
1½ tablespoons Worcestershire sauce
1 teaspoon celery salt
2 pounds lobster meat or crab
Dash cayenne pepper
½ cup cooking sherry
1 teaspoon fresh lemon juice
3 hard boiled eggs

Melt 2 tablespoons of butter in a large skillet. Add the lobster or crabmeat, already cooked, and sprinkle well with cayenne. Let cook until it sizzles but does not quite brown. Then adjust heat so it keeps warm without actually cooking. Melt the rest of the butter in another large kettle, blend in the flour and slowly stir in enough milk to make a smooth paste. Add the rest of the milk and cook, stirring until it thickens slightly, is smooth and well blended. Add Worcestershire sauce and a few drops of lemon juice to hot meat. Combine this with the milk mixture. Stir the cream that has been heated to a scald (in double boiler) and the sherry. If too thick, add a little more cream. Ladle into warm individual bowls. Sprinkle crumbled egg yolks on top and serve.

Serves 9 to 10   Mrs. Thomas Gardiner

The Abenaki Indian name for
Cherry Stone and Little Neck Clams is Quahaugs.

Fish and Seafood Stew

The types of fish may be varied. The stew goes well with rice or noodles.

3   tablespoons olive oil
1   pound plum tomatoes
½   pound sea scallops
¾   pound non-oily fish (haddock, cod, halibut)
2   teaspoons minced garlic
½   cup chopped onion
1   cup dry white wine
1   bay leaf
½   teaspoon hot green pepper

Cut fish into 1" cubes and tomatoes into ½" cubes. In heavy skillet heat oil and wilt onion and garlic. Add wine and cook briefly, adding tomatoes, bay leaf, peppers, and salt and pepper to taste. Bring to boil and simmer for 5 minutes. Add fish and stir. Cover and cook for 5 minutes. Remove bay leaf. Garnish with parsley.

Serves 4   Cecile Carver

Fish Stew Provençal

1   pound fillet of haddock
1   cup water
¾   cup finely chopped onion
1   garlic clove, finely chopped
1   tablespoon chives or scallions
1   tablespoon parsley
1   tomato, skinned and chopped
    (1 large or 2 small cans of
    tomatoes, drained, may be
    substituted)
2   tablespoons butter
2   teaspoons salt
⅛   teaspoon black pepper
⅛   teaspoon nutmeg
⅛   teaspoon thyme

⅛ teaspoon tarragon
½ teaspoon Worcestershire sauce
3 drops Tabasco sauce
3 cups skimmed milk
1 teaspoon grated lemon rind

Cut fish into four or five pieces and place in covered frying pan with water. Cover and simmer just until fish flakes. Remove fish from broth and retain broth. Melt butter in a small skillet and sauté onion, scallions or chives, and garlic until tender. Add to fish broth along with tomato and all the seasonings. Simmer 25 minutes. Add milk and lemon rind to broth. Return fish pieces to broth. Heat to serving temperature; do not boil.

Serves 4 to 6   Helen S. Small

Cold Buttermilk and Shrimp Soup

1 quart buttermilk
1 tablespoon dry mustard
1 teaspoon salt
1 teaspoon sugar
½ pound cooked shrimp, cooled, shelled, cleaned and finely chopped, reserving 2-3 halved lengthwise for garnish (optional)
1 cucumber, peeled, seeded and chopped fine, plus slices for garnish (optional)
2 tablespoons minced fresh chives

In large bowl, whisk buttermilk, mustard, salt and sugar. Add shrimp, cucumber and chives. Stir well. Chill soup, covered, 3 hours or until very cold. Makes about 5 cups.

Serves 4 to 6   Kate Debevoise

Fast & Easy Crab or Lobster Bisque

8   ounces crabmeat or lobster meat, cooked
¼   cup butter or margarine
2   teaspoons flour
1½ cups whole milk
1½ cups half and half
½   teaspoon Worcestershire sauce
½   teaspoon grated lemon rind
⅛   teaspoon ground mace
½   teaspoon salt
⅛   teaspoon white pepper
1   tablespoon cracker crumbs
2   tablespoons sherry
¼   cup whipping cream, whipped
    Freshly ground nutmeg

If frozen seafoods are used, thaw, and retain liquid. Use only cooked seafood, cut in chunks. Heat butter in top of double boiler over rapidly boiling water. Blend in flour. Add milk and half and half, slowly, stirring constantly. Add Worcestershire sauce, grated lemon rind, mace and seafood. Stir well and cook slowly for 20 minutes. Season with salt and white pepper. Add cracker crumbs. Stir well. Allow to stand for 10-15 minutes. Add sherry. Serve in heated bowls. Add a dollop of whipped cream and sprinkle with freshly ground nutmeg.

Serves 3 or 4   Donna Aldrich

Jon Legere's New England Crab Soup

In memory of my friend Edna Singles who so graciously gave me the basics of this recipe at the old Beckett Castle on Singles Road in Cape Elizabeth.

¼   pound butter (or margarine)
½   cup diced celery
½   cup diced onion
2   tablespoons flour
1   tablespoon dried parsley
1   tablespoon paprika

2   6-ounce containers fresh
crabmeat
2   dashes cayenne pepper
1   quart half and half
Paprika and chopped parsley for
garnish

In large sauté pan, at medium heat, melt butter (or margarine). Add celery, onion, dried parsley, paprika and cayenne pepper. Sauté until celery and onion just begin to brown. Add flour to roux consistency. Add crabmeat, stirring well until hot. Add half and half. Bring just to boiling point, and stir for 30 seconds. Remove from heat and let stand for 5 minutes. Serve in your best soup bowls with toast points on side. Garnish with dash of paprika and fresh chopped parsley.

Serves 6   Jon Legere
                                                                Artist

Squirrel Island Tea Shop Clam Chowder

Fresh clams may be substituted for the canned whole baby clams, but the minced clams should still be included.

3   cans whole baby clams
10 small red potatoes, cut into ¼"
    to ½" cubes, but not peeled
1   46-ounce can clam juice or broth
¼   teaspoon black pepper
3   cans minced clams
2   large onions, minced
3   to 4 strips cooked bacon
2   cans evaporated milk
2   tablespoons butter

Simmer cubed, unpeeled potatoes and minced onions in clam broth for ½ hour. Add clams, pepper and evaporated milk. Crumble in bacon. Float butter on top. When butter is completely melted, chowder is ready to serve.

Makes 12 cups or 6 bowls   Clare Newbury
                            Squirrel Island Tea Shop, Squirrel Island

Fish Chowder

Very easy, one pot meal. May be made a day ahead.

1 pound salt pork (fat back)
2 medium onions, diced
4 to 5 cups potatoes in 1" pieces
2 pounds fish fillets (haddock or cod)
1 to 2 cups water
½ to 1 teaspoon salt
¼ teaspoon pepper
3 cups whole milk
1 tall can evaporated milk
Crown Pilot Crackers

Remove rind from salt pork and cut into ¼" cubes (easier when pork is cold). Fry slowly in kettle until golden. Remove and drain on paper towels. Remove all but about 3 tablespoons of fat from kettle. Add onions and cook slowly until yellowed and soft, but not brown. Add potatoes and enough water so it comes nearly to top of potatoes. Place whole fish fillets on top. Sprinkle with salt and pepper. Cover, bring to a boil. Lower heat and simmer until potatoes are tender and the fish "flakes" (about 25 to 40 minutes). Add both kinds of milk and heat through but do not boil. If you stir at all, don't break up fish pieces. Pork scraps are served in a small dish and can be sprinkled on chowder as desired. Serve with warmed Crown Pilot Crackers.

Serves 4 to 8   Mary Sue Fisher

Haddock Oven Chowder

Wonderfully rich and soothing chowder! Serve with salad and a crusty French bread.

2 pounds haddock fillets
4 potatoes, peeled and diced
Few celery leaves, chopped
1 bay leaf
2 teaspoons salt
⅛ teaspoon ground cloves

1   clove of garlic, minced
3   medium onions, chopped
½   cup butter or margarine, melted
¼   teaspoon dill weed
¼   teaspoon white pepper
½   cup dry white wine
2   cups boiling water
2   cups half and half

Preheat oven to 350 degrees

Put all ingredients except cream into a large casserole. Cover and bake at 350 degrees for 1 hour, remove bay leaf. Heat cream to scalding and add to chowder. Stir to flake fish.

Serves 8 to 10   Ann Lane

Arno's Oyster Noodle

Every time it's superb!

1   pound fresh oysters
½   pound smoked salmon, diced
5   shallots, chopped
2   carrots, cut in julienne strips
3   leeks, cut in julienne strips
1   cup mushrooms, chopped
½   cup oyster juice
½   cup heavy cream
½   pound fine noodles
    Salt and pepper
2   cups white wine

Sauté chopped shallots in butter. Add carrots, leeks and mushrooms. Continue to sauté. Add oysters and salmon. Add dash of salt and pepper and wine. Simmer for 10 minutes, covered. Add oyster juice and heavy cream. Continue to simmer for 10 more minutes. Prepare noodles, combine all and serve.

Serves 4   Sally Trussell

Bouillabaisse à la Northeast

The seafood ingredients may be varied depending on the season and personal taste. Serve with fresh French bread. Have a large bowl on the table for discarding shells.

4	cups good fish broth (4 cups of clam juice may be substituted)
2	cups white wine
1	cup water
1	medium sized onion, sliced or chopped
3	cloves of garlic, crushed
3	carrots, shredded
3	medium sized tomatoes, sliced
1	teaspoon dry tarragon
	Salt and pepper
2	small lobsters
18	medium shrimp
18	scallops
18	clams
18	mussels
2	pounds white fish (haddock, flounder, sole, etc.)
2	tablespoons chopped parsley for garnish

In a large cooking pot, place the chopped onion, carrots, tomatoes, tarragon and garlic with the broth, wine and water. Bring everything to a boil. Reduce the heat and simmer for 45 minutes. At that point, cut the lobster in pieces and add to the pot, cooking for 5 minutes more. Then add the shrimp, scallops, clams and mussels, cooking another 5 minutes. Finally, add the fish, cooking for 5 minutes more. Serve in large soup bowls with a little parsley sprinkled on top.

Serves 6

Richard Estes
Artist

Bouillabaisse - French Fish Soup

Best to make a day in advance. Instant fish stock cubes may be purchased in gourmet section of supermarket.

3	pounds assorted fish: halibut, bass, cod, shrimp, lobster
4	tablespoons olive oil
1	onion
3	fresh tomatoes, skinned
3	leeks, white portion
1	tablespoon fennel
2	bay leaves
	Dash of celery seed
½	teaspoon saffron
4	tablespoons chopped parsley
2	teaspoons orange peel
3	to 4 cups fish stock
½	cup clamato juice, or more if needed

Heat oil in large casserole or deep pan. Add vegetables and herbs. Cook until soft. Cut up fish and add fish stock. Cook 10 minutes over medium flame and stir. Add additional seasoning. Serve in bowl with toasted French bread.

Serves 8   Phoebe White

*Make sure dried bay leaves
are green; if they are gray, there is no flavor left.*

Mussels Baked with Potatoes and Fresh Tomatoes

A flavorful Italian one-dish meal for a luncheon or an informal dinner. Follow it with a mixed salad and fresh fruit or ice cream.

3	pounds fresh mussels
1	pound potatoes
6	tablespoons olive oil
3	tablespoons parsley
1	tablespoon chopped garlic
¼	cup toasted unflavored bread crumbs
¼	cup grated Parmesan cheese
	Black pepper in a grinder
10	ounces fresh ripe plum tomatoes
	Salt

Preheat oven to 425 degrees

Soak mussels in a sink of cold water, scrubbing them and pulling away the beard. Continue to wash the mussels in at least 5 changes of clean, cold water using a stiff brush. Put the mussels in a tightly lidded pot without any water and turn the heat on high to medium high. As soon as the shells open, which may happen very quickly, drain the mussels and set them aside to cool. Wash the potatoes and boil them with their skins on. When the mussels have cooled enough to handle, detach the meat from the shell and put in a bowl. Add 3 tablespoons of the olive oil, chopped parsley, chopped garlic, 2 tablespoons of the bread crumbs, 2 tablespoons of the grated cheese, and several grindings of pepper. Mix well. Wash the tomatoes and skin them with a peeler (do not plunge them in boiling water; it would make them soggy). Cut them in half, lengthwise, remove the seeds, cut them lengthwise into ¼" wide strips and place them in a colander to drain. When potatoes are done, drain them, peel them and cut them into ¼ inch thick slices. It doesn't matter if the slices break a little. Choose a 13" x 9" oven-to-table baking dish and smear the bottom with 1 tablespoon of olive oil. Cover the bottom with a layer of potatoes, preferably without too much overlapping, but use up all the potatoes. Sprinkle with salt. Cover the potatoes with a layer of mussels and all the seasonings in their bowl. Sprinkle lightly with salt. Top with tomato strips. Do not add salt. Sprinkle with the rest of the bread crumbs and grated cheese. Pour over it the remaining olive oil in a thin, uniformly distributed stream. Bake in the uppermost level of the preheated oven until golden brown, about 10-15 minutes. Remove from the oven and allow to settle for at least 5 minutes before serving.

Serves 4 to 6   Sandy Potholm

Broiled Herbed Mussels

This is a delicious one, but don't skimp on butter!

30 to 35 fresh mussels, scrubbed
     clean
¾ pound (3 sticks) butter, softened
6 shallots, finely minced
4 cloves garlic, finely minced
1⅓ cups day-old dry bread crumbs
3 tablespoons minced parsley
     Salt and pepper to taste

Preheat oven to 450 degrees

Arrange mussels on baking sheet(s) and place in preheated 450 degree oven for 7 or 8 minutes until shells open. Discard any unopened shells. Remove and cool. Blend 3 sticks softened butter with 6 finely minced shallots, garlic, bread crumbs, parsley, salt and pepper. Remove and discard top shells of mussels and spread each mussel with generous amounts of butter mixture and chill for 30 minutes. Broil under pre-heated broiler for 3-4 minutes or until crumbs are golden.

Serves 4 as first course.   John Muench
                                                                      Artist

*To reduce high sodium count in
pimento-stuffed olives, rinse thoroughly.*

Mussels à la Roberto

Even though this is labor intensive, it will be worth it!

5   pounds bearded mussels
½   pound plum tomatoes, either
    fresh or canned, chopped
    Parsley
    Head of garlic, chopped
½   bottle white wine
    Sprinkle hot pepper
    Fennel seeds
    Bay leaf
    Drizzle olive oil (extra virgin)

Steam mussels in ½ bottle wine, pepper, spices, and olive oil. Pour into colander. Let cool and break off ½ shell, leaving "boats" with mussels in them. Fill up with chopped tomatoes, garlic and a dab of olive oil. Bake for 10 minutes at 350 degrees.

Serves 4   Brita Holmquist
                                                  Artist

Maine Lobster with Basil and Vanilla

4   1½-pound live lobsters
1   clove garlic, peeled and chopped
1   rib celery, diced
1   leek, white part only, split,
    cleaned and diced
1   medium carrot, diced
1   sprig each of parsley, thyme, and
    tarragon plus two bay leaves,
    tied with cotton twine
6   peppercorns, crushed
1   tablespoon vegetable oil
2   vanilla beans
¼   pound unsalted butter
1   cup dry white wine

1   cup fresh basil leaves, loosely
     packed
2   tablespoons Cognac brandy
     Salt and cayenne pepper to taste
     Basil leaves for decoration

In a large pot or Dutch oven, heat the vegetable oil, add the vegetables, herb bouquet and peppercorns. Cook the mixture over moderate heat 4 or 5 minutes, or until vegetables begin to soften. Add the white wine, boil, then simmer one minute. Remove the rubber bands from the 4 lobsters and place them on their backs in the pot. Increase the heat and cover the pot tightly. Cook 7 minutes, timing from the commencement of boiling. Turn off the heat and remove the lobsters. Cool. Remove the meat carefully from tails, knuckles, and claws. Reserve the bodies and legs for another use. Keep the lobster meat cool. Split the vanilla beans lengthwise. Scrape out the tar-like seeds with the blunt edge of a paring knife and add the seeds to the workbowl of a food processor (save the split bean shells). Add the butter and process until the mixture is smooth and the vanilla seeds are distributed. Strain the lobster cooking liquid into a wide, non-corroding skillet, pressing down on the solids. Add the split vanilla beans, each cut in half. Rapidly boil the mixture down until ¾ cup remains. Reduce the heat to a bare simmer. Whisk in the butter by tablespoons, incorporating completely. Add the Cognac. Adjust the seasoning with a pinch of cayenne and salt, if necessary. Slice the basil leaves across their length into thin shreds (called chiffonnade in the trade) and add the basil to the sauce. Heat the lobster meat gently in the sauce—do not let the sauce boil or it may separate. Divide the lobster among four serving plates. Spoon the sauce over the lobster. Decorate with additional whole basil leaves and the pieces of vanilla bean.

Serves 4   Sam Hayward, Chef and Food Manager
                                                  Harraseeket Inn, Freeport

To keep yogurt from separating in cooking, have it at room temperature, cook at low temperature for as short a time as possible, and fold rather than stir in.

Baked Stuffed Lobster

Fantastic! May be made ahead of time and reheated.

6   live 1¼-pound lobsters
    Meat from 1-pound cooked
    lobster (for stuffing)
¼   pound raw shrimp
½   pound butter
½   pound crabmeat
½   pound scallops, cut into pieces
35 Ritz crackers, crushed
1½ tablespoons Worcestershire
    sauce
    Pepper to taste
    Paprika

Preheat oven to 400 degrees

Cook lobsters in boiling salted water for 10 minutes. Remove and let cool. Sauté peeled shrimp in butter. Add cooked meat from 1-pound lobster, crab and scallops and heat through. Mix in cracker crumbs, Worcestershire sauce and pepper. Turn lobsters on their backs. Insert knife at head of each and quickly split from head to tail, as far as you can go. Spread open and remove small hard sac just below head by hooking finger under it. Stuff lobsters with crumb mixture and sprinkle with paprika. Bake on rimmed cookie sheet in preheated 400 degree oven for 25 minutes.

Serves 6

Grilled Lobster Sandwich

Make lobster salad, mixing small pieces of lobster with mayonnaise and a touch of fresh lemon juice. Butter one side of bread. Spread lobster between the unbuttered slices. Put in a sauté pan on low heat until bread is grilled to a golden brown. Then turn over and do the other side.

Peg Dinan

Lobster Casserole

Delicious. Fine made day ahead and left in refrigerator. Flavor improves.

4	tablespoons butter
4	tablespoons flour
2	cups milk or light cream
1	teaspoon salt
½	teaspoon pepper
2	tablespoons sherry
½	teaspoon celery seed
	Dash cayenne pepper
1	teaspoon minced onion
1	teaspoon minced parsley
1	egg yolk
1	cup sliced fresh mushrooms
4	cups cooked lobster meat, sautéed in butter (crab, scallops and shrimp may be added for seafood casserole, but not to exceed 4 cups)
2	cups bread crumbs
	Parmesan cheese and butter

Preheat oven to 400 degrees

Melt butter in saucepan. Blend in flour. Cook over low heat. Add milk (cream). Stir constantly until smooth and thick. Remove from heat. Add egg and stir briskly. Add mushrooms, onions, sherry, lobster, parsley and seasonings. Pour in large casserole. Sprinkle with crumbs and cheese. Dot with butter. Bake uncovered in 400 degree oven for 20 to 25 minutes.

Serves 8   Manny Morgan

One tablespoon of cornstarch, arrowroot, or potato starch has the thickening power of 2 tablespoons of flour.

Lobster Mornay

This is an exquisite recipe, a nice change from "boiled" or "stuffed" lobster.

2 pounds fresh cooked lobster meat, chopped in big, bite-sized pieces
6 tablespoons butter
3 tablespoons flour
¼ teaspoon ground pepper
1 teaspoon salt
2 cups milk
1 egg yolk, slightly beaten
1½ cups shredded sharp Cheddar cheese

Preheat oven to 350 degrees

Melt butter, add flour, and bubble nicely for a few minutes but do not scorch. When smooth, add seasonings. Slowly add milk, stirring until thickened. Pull from heat and add a bit of the hot sauce to the egg yolk. Add egg mixture to the rest of the sauce. Return to heat for a minute or two, stirring steadily. Remove from heat. Add the lobster meat to the sauce and mix thoroughly. Divide evenly into six buttered ramekins, or pour into buttered baking dish. Evenly spread the shredded cheese over all. Bake at 350 degrees until hot and bubbly.

Serves 6

Mary Haggerty
Lincoln House Country Inn, Dennysville

Seafood Aspic

This is a good "fix-it-ahead" aspic.

1 can tomato soup
3 3-ounce packages cream cheese
3 envelopes gelatin
1 cup cold water
1 cup mayonnaise

1½ cups cooked shrimp or lobster
meat
¼ cup chopped onion
½ cup chopped green peppers
1 cup chopped celery
1 teaspoon salt
2 tablespoons lemon juice
Dash of Worcestershire sauce

Heat cheese and soup together in double boiler. Add gelatin after softening in cold water. Add mayonnaise and beat in electric mixer until smooth. Stir in remaining ingredients. Pour into oiled 1½-quart mold. Chill several hours. Unmold onto bed of lettuce and serve.

Serves 8   Beth Wiggins

Claremont Seafood Thermidor

This is very rich and substitutes do not work very well. More cream may be necessary if dish seems too dry. Too much is better than not enough.

½ pound haddock
½ pound scallops
½ pound crabmeat
1 cup melted butter
1 cup crushed saltines
1 cup cubed soft bread
1 pint medium cream
Salt and pepper

Preheat oven to 350 degrees

Add butter to crackers and bread, mix well. Put a layer of crumbs in baking dish. Layer seafood and sprinkle with salt and pepper. Cover with remaining crumbs. Pour cream over all. Bake for 45 minutes at 350 degrees.

Serves 4 to 6   Billie McIntire, Chef
Claremont Hotel, Southwest Harbor

Down East Casserole

12	ounces thin noodles
1	pound scallops, quartered
1	pound Maine shrimp
1	cup butter
6	tablespoons flour
⅛	teaspoon salt
½	teaspoon pepper
4	cups milk (if desired, substitute some of milk with liquor from fish)
¾	pound fresh mushrooms
½	to ⅔ cup sherry
½	pound sharp American cheese, grated
	Paprika

Preheat oven to 350 degrees

Cook noodles and drain. Sauté scallops in 4 tablespoons butter. When almost cooked, add shrimp and cook until seafood is opaque. Drain and save liquid. Melt 6 tablespoons butter and blend in flour, salt and pepper. Cook until smooth. Slowly add milk and cook until sauce thickens, stirring constantly. Add sherry. Add scallops, shrimp and sauce to noodles. In remaining 6 tablespoons of butter, sauté thinly sliced mushrooms over medium heat until tender. Add to noodles mixture. Top with cheese. Cover and bake 45 minutes at 350 degrees. Sprinkle with paprika and place under broiler for 3 minutes or until top is brown and bubbly.

Serves 8   Mrs. Richard C. Britton

Elegant Scalloped Scallops

Easy. May be assembled ahead of time, omitting the cream until the last minute.

¾	cup margarine or butter (unsalted o.k.)
2	cups Ritz cracker crumbs

1   cup soft bread crumbs
1½ pounds sea scallops
1½ cups light cream or half and half
2   teaspoons paprika
1   tablespoon chopped parsley

Preheat oven to 350 degrees

Butter baking dish. Melt butter over low heat and mix well with crumbs. Spread ⅓ of the crumbs on the bottom of the dish, add ½ the scallops, add another layer of crumbs, then the rest of the scallops. Top with the rest of the crumbs, pour in the cream and sprinkle with the paprika and parsley. Bake 30-40 minutes at 350 degrees until scallops are cooked through and bubbling.

Serves 6   Mrs. G. S. Gould

Scallop Linguine

1 pound cooked lobster may be substituted for scallops and sherry may be substituted for the wine.

1   tablespoon butter
2   tablespoons olive oil
½   cup chopped onion (Vidalia in season)
2   cloves garlic, minced
1   tablespoon flour
¼   cup dry white wine
1   cup cream
½   to ¾ pound scallops, washed well (if scallops are large, cut in half)
1   pound cooked linguine

Sauté onion and garlic in oil and butter. Stir in flour. Add wine and cream and bring to a boil. Stir until slightly thickened. Add scallops and simmer until cooked through, about 5 minutes (do not overcook). Serve over cooked linguine.

Serves 4   LuAnn Perakis

Scallops

1 pound sea scallops
1 tablespoon butter
1½ teaspoons lemon or lime juice
½ teaspoon Tabasco

Wash and drain scallops, don't bother to dry. Heat non-stick skillet to medium high. Place scallops in hot, dry skillet. Let cook, maybe 5 minutes, or until golden brown. Turn scallops to other flat side. Turn down heat to medium low. When both sides are done, turn heat up, add butter and shake pan to loosen. Add lemon juice and shake again. Add Tabasco, toss and serve.

Serves 2 to 3   Nick Witte

Salmon Cakes with Fresh Pea Sauce

There is a long standing tradition of serving salmon and peas together on the Fourth of July.

Salmon Cakes:
1½ pounds salmon fillet, skinned
6 scallions, chopped fine
2 tablespoons fresh ginger, minced
1 egg, lightly beaten
1 tablespoon fresh lemon juice
1 teaspoon soy sauce
Salt and pepper to taste
¼ cup vegetable oil or more if necessary
Fresh Pea Sauce:
2 tablespoons minced shallots
3 tablespoons unsalted butter
1 cup dry white wine
2½ cups heavy cream
3 cups fresh peas, coarsely chopped
1 teaspoon lemon juice
Salt and pepper to taste

    3   tablespoons fresh chopped mint, optional

Pea Sauce: sauté the shallots in the butter in a large saucepan. Add the wine and reduce by half over medium high heat. Add the heavy cream and continue cooking until slightly thickened, about 15 minutes. Add the chopped peas and simmer another 5-7 minutes until thickened to desired consistency. Add lemon, salt and pepper to taste, and the optional mint. To serve, spoon sauce over the cakes on the platter or transfer to individual heated dinner plates.

Preheat oven to 200 degrees

Salmon Cakes: chop the salmon coarsely with a knife (using a food processor for this will give the cakes a mealy texture). In a large bowl, mix the salmon with the remaining ingredients except the oil. Shape into 12 patties and set aside. When ready to cook them, heat one tablespoon of vegetable oil in a large nonstick pan. Working in batches, sauté the cakes until lightly browned on both sides, about 3 minutes. Add oil to pan as needed. Drain cakes on paper towels. Transfer to a heat-proof platter and keep warm in the oven for up to 30 minutes.

Serves 6

                                  Cheryl Lewis and Norine Kotts
                                       Cafe Always, Portland

Salmon Marguerita

    Fresh salmon
    4   to 5 tablespoons fresh lime juice
    4   to 5 tablespoons tequila
    3   to 4 tablespoons unsalted butter

Preheat oven to 425 degrees

Oven poach fresh salmon at 425 degrees for 12 to 15 minutes. Combine lime juice and tequila and reduce by half. Whisk in butter. Serve over salmon. Garnish with fresh lime.

                                      Suzanne Uhl-Myers, Chef
                                      Lake House, Waterford

BG's Simple Salmon

Quick. Everyone likes it.

Salmon:
>Filet of salmon (check for bones)
>Lemon juice
>Salt and pepper to taste
>Dill
>Heavy duty foil

Dill Sauce:
1   cup sour cream
1   lemon, juiced
2   green onions, chopped
½   teaspoon dill

Preheat oven to 350 degrees

Salmon: place fillet on buttered foil. Add lemon juice, salt, pepper and dill. Seal foil and bake at 350 degrees for 20-25 minutes. Remove from oven and place on serving platter.

Dill Sauce: combine ingredients in a small saucepan. Heat until just warm. Serve salmon with this dill sauce or with Hollandaise sauce.

Joan R. Shepherd

Deviled Crabmeat

1   container fresh crabmeat
     (or 1 can)
1½ cups milk
1   tablespoon chopped onions
1½ tablespoons chopped celery
½   pound mushrooms, sliced
2   tablespoons butter
3   tablespoons flour
¼   teaspoon mustard
1   teaspoon salt
     Pepper
     Bread crumbs

Grated Cheddar cheese
Lemon slices, optional

Preheat oven to 350 degrees

Put butter in frying pan, add vegetables, and stir. Cook until onion is yellow. Then add flour, mustard, salt and pepper. Blend well and add milk, stirring until thick. Add crabmeat to the mixture and fill large casserole or individual casseroles which have been buttered. Cover the tops with buttered crumbs mixed with grated cheese. Bake at 350 degrees for 25 minutes. Garnish with lemon slices.

Serves 4   Margaret Sowles

Crab Mousse

Velvet smooth and simple to prepare. Delicious served with hot biscuits.

2   tablespoons gelatin
¼   cup diluted vinegar, white wine variety preferred (½ water and ½ vinegar)
1   cup clam or chicken broth, boiling
1   cup diced cucumbers
1½   cups fresh crabmeat (¾ pound)
1   teaspoon Worcestershire sauce
1   cup sour cream
½   small can water chestnuts, sliced
2   tablespoons capers

Soften gelatin in diluted vinegar. In container of an electric blender (or food processor) put gelatin, vinegar and broth. Cover and blend one minute. Add cucumber, crabmeat and Worcestershire sauce. Blend one minute more. Remove from blender (processor) and stir in sour cream, water chestnuts and capers. Pour into a 1-quart mold and chill until firm. Unmold and serve on a bed of watercress.

Serves 4   Barbara Y. Sturgeon

Crabcakes

1   small egg, beaten
2   tablespoons mayonnaise
1   teaspoon yellow mustard
1   teaspoon Worcestershire sauce
    Juice of ½ lemon
½   teaspoon celery seed
1   to 2 teaspoons Old Bay
    seasoning (to taste)
1   pound crabmeat
    Bread crumbs as needed

Preheat oven to broil

Mix all ingredients in a bowl in order. Add crabmeat after draining and drying. Form palm-sized crabcakes, makes 6. Use light bread crumbs to absorb excess moisture. Broil in oven, or toaster oven, for 20 minutes or fry in pan with butter. Turn once.

Serves 3   Stuart Karu
                                                Trustee

Swordfish in Sour Cream

Swordfish must be fresh to have this dish taste best.

2   to 3 pounds swordfish steak,
    1½" thick
2   to 3 tablespoons butter
½   lime, sliced thin
1   pint sour cream
    Fresh dill
    Lemon quarters

Preheat oven to broil

Place dabs of butter on top of swordfish and place under broiler until slightly browned. Place half slices of lime on top and return to broiler for more browning. Adjust oven to bake at 350 degrees. Thin sour cream by adding milk, if desired, and mix in snips of fresh dill. Put swordfish in baking dish (rectangular or oblong) and pour sour cream mixture on top. Cover with aluminum foil. Bake 30-35 minutes at 350 degrees. Serve with lemon quarters and sprinkle with fresh dill.

Serves 4   Charlotte Brown

Grilled Swordfish with Pesto Butter

Extra pesto butter is wonderful on French bread.

Fish:
- 1½ to 2 pounds swordfish steaks
- Salt and pepper to taste
- 2 tablespoons olive oil
- 1 tablespoon lemon juice

Pesto Butter:
- 6 tablespoons butter
- ½ cup fresh basil leaves
- ⅓ cup grated Parmesan cheese
- 2 cloves garlic

Let swordfish stand in lemon juice and olive oil for 15 minutes. Sprinkle with pepper and salt on both sides. Meanwhile, make pesto butter by placing butter, basil, cheese and garlic in food processor. Process until smooth. Grill swordfish until cooked through. Serve steaks topped with pesto butter.

Serves 4   Peggy Haughey

Blend sour cream and capers and
spread on fish before baking.

Swordfish Sauce

Easy and absolutely delicious!

1 egg, beaten
2 tablespoons dill weed
1 teaspoon salt
Pinch ground pepper
Pinch sugar
4 teaspoons fresh lemon juice
1 teaspoon grated onion
1½ cups sour cream

Beat egg until fluffy and lemon colored. Add remaining ingredients except sour cream. Fold in sour cream at the end and chill. Enjoy!

Serves 10 to 12   Didi Washburn

New Meadows River Fish Hash

An unforgettable part of growing up in Maine was the memorable breakfasts at Grandmother Drake's. A special event was Fish Hash, hot biscuits or popovers and crabapple jelly, a typical Scottish-English coastal breakfast.

1 large fillet of sole, haddock, cod or hake
2 medium onions
4 medium potatoes
White pepper and salt, to taste

Sauté onions in iron skillet until tender. Boil potatoes in salted water, drain, mash and add to onions in skillet. Cook fish in small amount of salted water, usually done at first boil. Remove from pan and flake with the touch of a fork. Drain and add fish to skillet. Reserve fish stock for future gastronomic adventures. Salt and pepper to taste. Melt butter in fry pan and cook on each side, turning hash when one side is golden and crispy.

Serves 4

Fish Mousse

Excellent hot or cold weather dish for first course, lunch or dinner.

Fish Mousse:
1½ pounds fillet of sole
¾ pound salmon
1 pound scallops
1 teaspoon salt
¼ teaspoon white pepper
¼ teaspoon cayenne pepper
2 tablespoons brandy
1 clove garlic, mashed
4 eggs, separated
2 tablespoons gelatin softened in 3 tablespoons water
2 cups whipping cream

Sour Cream Dill Sauce:
1 cup sour cream
½ to ¾ cup Hellmann's mayonnaise
2 to 3 tablespoons good olive oil Lemon juice to taste
¼ cup chopped fresh dill or to taste

Sauce: mix all ingredients. Make several hours before serving to blend flavors.

Preheat oven to 350 degrees

Mousse: in a food processor, process fillets for 30 seconds. Add egg yolks, gelatin, brandy, seasonings, garlic, 1 cup of cream and process 30 seconds. Add scallops, process a few seconds but keep some lumps. Whip second cup of cream until stiff. Whip egg whites until stiff, not dry, and fold all together with fish mixture. Pour into an oiled 8-cup loaf pan, cover with buttered aluminum foil. Place in bain marie (pan of hot water) with water half way up loaf pan sides. Bake for 45 minutes at 350 degrees. Cool, cover with plastic wrap and cool overnight in refrigerator. Unmold by dipping in hot water. Mousse will keep for 3 days, refrigerated.

Serves 12 to 14   Patricia R. Pratt

Sole Adelaide

This is very easy to do. It can be assembled several hours ahead and refrigerated.

1   package spinach soufflé, thawed
1   pound fillet of flounder
⅔   cup sour cream
⅓   cup mayonnaise
     Parmesan cheese
     Paprika
1   teaspoon dried tarragon

Preheat oven to 350 degrees

Thaw the spinach soufflé and cover the bottom of a 9" x 12" baking dish. Put flounder on top of spinach. Mix sour cream and mayonnaise. Spread over fish, covering completely. Sprinkle Parmesan cheese, 1 teaspoon tarragon and paprika on top of cream mixture. Bake at 350 degrees, uncovered, for 30 minutes.

Serves 4   Jane H. Heizmann

Fish Florentine

May be put together earlier in the day and baked just before serving.

2   pounds haddock (sole or perch
     may be used)
1   package fresh spinach, washed
     and cooked
3   large fresh tomatoes, sliced (well
     drained canned tomatoes may be
     substituted)
     Pepperidge Farm Seasoned
     Stuffing

Preheat oven to 375 degrees

Line lightly greased shallow casserole dish with well drained cooked spinach. Layer haddock fillets on spinach. Slice tomatoes and layer on haddock. Sprinkle Pepperidge Farm Stuffing over all. Bake 30 minutes at 375 degrees.

Serves 6 to 8   Verna Andrews

Poached Flounder

Could use other white fish fillets. Poaching time differs according to the thickness of fillet.

> 6 flounder fillets
>   Flour mixed with salt and
>   pepper for coating
> 1 tablespoon butter
> 1 teaspoon chopped onion
> 1 can consommé
> ½ cup sherry
> 1 bay leaf
> 1 teaspoon chopped parsley
> 1 stalk celery, chopped
> 2 tablespoons heavy cream
>   Parmesan cheese

Preheat oven to 350 degrees

Dip fish in flour (mixed with salt and pepper), both sides. Melt butter in fry pan and add 1 teaspoon chopped onion until softened. Put in fish, consommé, sherry, bay leaf, chopped parsley and chopped celery. Poach until tender, 10 minutes. Remove and put in shallow baking dish. Reduce liquid to 1½ cups. Pour over fish. Pour 2 tablespoons cream over fish. Sprinkle with Parmesan cheese. Place in 350 degree oven for 15 minutes or until brown on top.

Serves 6   Alice Wallis

Grilled Tuna with Basil and Capers

4   6-ounce tuna steaks, ¾" thick
3   tablespoons extra virgin olive oil
1   bunch fresh basil
1   lemon
2   teaspoons capers
    Szechuan peppercorns (optional)
    Black peppercorns
    Extra virgin olive oil

Brush tuna steaks lightly with olive oil. Mix Szechuan and black peppercorns in equal proportions; grind over tuna steaks as desired. Set steaks aside. Wash, stem and coarsely chop the basil. Mix with 3 tablespoons of extra virgin olive oil and the juice of one lemon. Add 2 teaspoons of capers. Let sit ½ hour. Add salt to taste. Grill tuna over very hot coals. Cook briefly; best flavor is when there is a thin strip of very rare meat in the center of the steak. Top with basil/caper mixture and serve immediately.

Serves 4   Leslie Otten
                                    President of the Board of Trustees

Baked Haddock in Sour Cream and Dill Sauce

2   pounds haddock
2   cups sour cream
½   cup mayonnaise
1   teaspoon celery salt
½   teaspoon pepper, freshly ground
¼   teaspoon thyme
½   teaspoon paprika
2   tablespoons diced pimento,
    drained
1   teaspoon dried dill or 2
    tablespoons fresh dill

Preheat oven to 350 degrees

Place haddock in buttered baking dish. Combine all other ingredients and mix well. Pour over fish. Bake at 350 degrees for 30-40 minutes or until fish is just done. Garnish with lemon and fresh dill.

Serves 6   Mary Haggerty
                        Lincoln House Country Inn, Dennysville

Mustard Dill Sauce For All Kinds of Grilled Fresh Fish

4   tablespoons Dijon-type mustard
1   teaspoon powdered mustard
3   tablespoons sugar
2   tablespoons white vinegar
⅓   cup vegetable oil
3   tablespoons chopped fresh dill

In the blender or a small deep bowl, mix the two mustards, sugar and vinegar to a paste. Slowly beat in oil until it thickens. Stir in fresh dill. May be made ahead and refrigerated. Double for a large party.

Serves 6 to 8   Judy Glickman

Baked Shrimp

20 large shrimp, uncooked
1½ packages Ritz crackers
    (4 packages to box)
½   cup dry vermouth or good dry
    white wine
2   sticks melted butter or
    margarine

Preheat oven to 350 degrees

Roll crackers into medium crumbs. Combine with wine and butter. Arrange shrimp in buttered casserole and cover with crumb mixture (may be done ahead). Bake at 350 degrees for 30 minutes or until top is golden and shrimp tender. Cooked shrimp may not take as long. Dressing protects shrimp from dryness, so a few minutes additional cooking will do no harm.

Serves 6 to 8

Shrimp Supreme

2 cups or more cooked shrimp
1 cup mushrooms, chopped
2 tablespoons butter or margarine
1 medium onion, chopped
2 to 3 tomatoes, peeled and seeded
2 tablespoons instant flour
1 cup light cream
¼ cup sweet sherry
½ teaspoon salt
¼ teaspoon pepper
½ cup buttered crumbs

Preheat oven to 350 degrees

Sauté mushrooms in butter. Add onion and tomatoes. Cook over low heat 10 minutes. Mix flour with cream to make a smooth paste. Add to mixture. Season with sherry, salt and pepper. Cook until sauce thickens. Add shrimp. Place in casserole. Cover with buttered crumbs. Bake at 350 degrees for 20 minutes. Serve with rice.

Serves 4   Georgiana Chase

Dutch Codfish Casserole

Guests love this. The codfish is greatly enhanced by the other ingredients.

1 pound cod fillets
1 tablespoon wine vinegar
4 sprigs parsley
  Salt and pepper
1½ pounds potatoes
¾ cup warm milk
½ cup butter
  Freshly ground nutmeg
2 medium onions, sliced
3 tablespoon flour
¼ cup prepared mustard

¼   teaspoon paprika
2   tablespoons lemon juice
⅓   cup Edam cheese, cubed

Preheat oven to 350 degrees

Put fish, vinegar, parsley, salt and pepper, and 1½ cups water in a saucepan. Simmer 10 minutes. Remove fish. Strain and reserve 1½ cups liquid. Break fish in small pieces. Peel potatoes. Boil until tender. Drain and mash while warm, add warm milk, 2 tablespoons butter, salt, pepper and nutmeg. Beat until fluffy. Sauté onions until tender in 3 tablespoons butter. Set aside. Melt 2 tablespoons butter in saucepan, stir in flour. Add fish stock and cook, stirring until sauce thickens. Stir in mustard, paprika, salt and pepper. Bring to boil. Remove from heat. Caution: to have fairly thick sauce, go easy on the liquid. Arrange ½ fish, ½ onions in buttered casserole dish. Sprinkle with 1 tablespoon lemon juice. Cover with ½ of the mustard sauce and ½ mashed potato. Repeat layers with potatoes on top. Dot with butter and cheese. Bake 30 minutes at 350 degrees. Slip under broiler during last minutes until bubbly.

Serves 6

Gigi Stewart

New England Codfish Balls

A favorite treat for Sunday morning breakfast at Oakland House. We serve 3 golden fish balls with chunks of corn bread and crisp bacon.

¼   pound dried salt codfish
6   potatoes, cooked, drained and mashed
3   eggs
1   cup bread crumbs

Cook cod in water until it flakes well; rinse with fresh water several times and drain well. In mixer blend potatoes and fish. Add eggs and bread crumbs to form a proper consistency for making into balls. Chill over night. Form into balls (a #40 ice cream scoop works well) and drop into 350 degree cooking oil in a deep fat frying pan until golden brown.

Makes about 24

Jim Littlefield
Oakland House, Sargentville

Cod Fish Fillets with Soy Sauce Dressing

*This is Chinese traditional fish cooking. Simple, elegant and delicious.
We serve this with cooked rice and with a Chinese vegetable dish such as
green beans in Hoisin Sauce.*

Sauce:
3   tablespoons soy sauce
     (Kikkoman)
2   tablespoons Shao Hsing wine
     (bought at any Asian food store)
     or very dry sherry
1   tablespoon high grade sesame
     seed oil
Fish:
4   match sticks slices fresh ginger
     (must be fresh), will amount to
     about ½ cup
2   green onions (including top
     green part), julienne
2   pounds cod fillets, can be
     haddock also
     Bunch of cilantro (coriander)

Sauce: place sauce ingredients in a small saucepan, ready to boil.
Fish: boil water in a wide frying pan (the widest) with a little ginger and
onion to add flavor. The water should be a depth of 2 to 3 inches,
enough to cover the fish when they are cooking. Reduce heat so hot
water barely simmers. Add fish, cover and simmer for 5 minutes or until
fish turns opaque. Do not boil. Lift out fish VERY GENTLY with a slotted
spatula and place on serving platter. Cover with ginger and one half side
with onion, the other side with cilantro. Bring sauce to a boil. Do not
burn. Drizzle sauce over the dish. Serve immediately.

Serves 4   Toshiyuki Shimada
Music Director & Conductor, Portland Symphony Orchestra
Eva Virsik-Shimada
Concert pianist

Poultry and Meats

McLellan-Sweat House
dining room mantle detail

New Simple Chicken with Sesame Seeds

Delicious! Light, interesting, simple.

1	tablespoon Dijon mustard
⅛	cup Tamari sauce
¼	cup extra virgin or other olive oil
1	teaspoon basil, minced, fresh preferred
2	whole chicken breasts, skinned, boned, halved
	Sesame seeds

Mix mustard, Tamari, basil and oil together. Pour enough in bottom of baking dish just to cover. Spoon rest over chicken, adding fresh ground pepper, if desired. Marinate several hours. Sprinkle top of chicken pieces with sesame seeds. Bake at 350 degrees a full half hour to 40 minutes, depending on how much chicken in dish. Do not overcook.

Mrs. William Hickey

Pesto Stuffed Chicken

This is easy to make and really good with a pasta salad.

2	large chicken breasts, split
½	cup pesto (basil/garlic/olive oil)
½	cup ricotta cheese
	Salt and pepper

Preheat oven to 400 degrees

Slip your fingers under the skin of each chicken breast, making a good place for the stuffing. Place in a shallow roasting pan. Divide the ricotta into 4 equal portions. Place a portion under each chicken skin. Spoon an equal amount of pesto under each chicken skin. Carefully pat the skin from above to evenly distribute the stuffing. Sprinkle with salt and pepper. Bake at 400 degrees for about an hour.

Serves 4

Lemon Chicken

A nice simple-to-make chicken dish.

Medium chicken, cut into pieces
½ cup butter
1 tablespoon sherry
2 tablespoons dry white wine
3 tablespoons grated Swiss cheese
Grated peel of 1 lemon
Grated peel of 1 orange
2 tablespoons lemon juice
1½ cups heavy cream

Sauté chicken in butter, slowly, covered, until done. Put in casserole. To sauté pan (add more butter, if necessary) add sherry and wine, grated peels, juice, salt and pepper. Turn up fire and add cream slowly. Pour over chicken, add cheese and lemon slices. Brown under boiler and serve.

Serves 4

Chicken Sauté with Oranges and Avocados

For that very special dinner. Sure to impress.

6 whole chicken breasts, boneless and skinned
3 tablespoons butter
2 tablespoons canola oil
¾ cup orange juice
⅓ cup dry white wine
½ cup sliced fresh mushrooms
2 tablespoons minced fresh parsley
1 teaspoon grated orange peel
Pinch of rosemary
3 tablespoons raspberry vinegar
2 oranges, peeled and sectioned
2 avocados, sliced

Pound chicken to flatten to even thickness. Dredge lightly with flour. Heat butter with oil in heavy skillet over medium high heat, add chicken and sauté until brown. Add orange juice, wine, mushrooms, parsley, orange peel and rosemary. Simmer for 8 minutes. Transfer chicken to heated dish. Add vinegar to skillet and continue to simmer, scraping up any browned bits until sauce is reduced about ⅓. Pour sauce over chicken. Garnish with orange sections and avocado slices.

Serves 6   Maryetta Bennett

Chicken Pockets

Great for leftover chicken and rice!

2	cups cold chicken, cooked and skinned
2	cups cooked rice
1	medium onion, chopped
	Sprig parsley, chopped
½	teaspoon bouquet garni
	Dash of pepper and salt to taste
2	tablespoons butter
2	tablespoons milk
	Puff pastry, frozen

Preheat oven to 350 degrees

Sauté onions, herbs and parsley until light. Add milk and seasonings. Chop chicken fine or "wiz" in food processor. Mix in rice with chicken and all seasoning. Mix well. Roll out puff pastry, slightly. Cut into square for triangles 6" square, or rectangle. Place ½ cup or more filling in center. Seal edges. Chill, if doing ahead of time. Bake 45 minutes at 350 degrees until golden brown. (Mushrooms may be added as may other vegetables. When adding vegetables, they should be slightly cooked, well drained and cool).

Serves 4   Elizabeth A. Hall-Baker

Apricot Chicken

This is my children's favorite dish and only has 215 calories per serving!

8   breast halves, skinned and boned chicken
½   cup flour
½   cup apricot preserves
1   tablespoon Dijon mustard
½   cup nonfat yogurt
2   tablespoons slivered almonds

Preheat oven to 375 degrees

Shake chicken in a plastic bag with flour to coat. Place chicken in a single layer in a shallow baking pan and bake for 25 minutes. Combine apricot preserves, mustard and yogurt. Spread mixture on chicken and bake for 10-15 minutes longer until bubbly. Brown almonds in toaster oven and sprinkle over chicken. Serve with rice.

Serves 8

Ann Willauer
President of the Museum Guild

Orange Chicken Tarragon

1   tablespoon orange zest
1   cup orange juice
¼   cup lemon juice
⅓   cup honey
2   tablespoons Worcestershire sauce
1   tablespoon tarragon (fresh or dried)
1   teaspoon dry mustard
   Salt and pepper
4   chicken breasts, whole, boneless
2   tablespoons cornstarch, dissolved in water

Preheat oven to 350 degrees

Combine first 7 ingredients. Pour over chicken and marinate, covered, for 2 hours in refrigerator. Bring to room temperature and place chicken and marinade in flat baking dish. Bake covered at 350 degrees for about 30 minutes. Thicken sauce with cornstarch and ladle over chicken when serving.

Serves 4 to 6   Rachel F. Armstrong
Chairman of the Board of Trustees

Chicken Tandoori

Delicious and easy to prepare! Watch out for the turmeric sauce. It will stain fabric.

2 pounds skinless chicken breasts
½ cup flour
Salad oil
1 medium onion, cubed
¼ cup plain yogurt
2 tablespoons lemon juice
1½ teaspoons salt (optional)
1½ teaspoons ground coriander
1 teaspoon sugar
¾ teaspoon ginger
¾ teaspoon turmeric
¼ teaspoon ground pepper

Cut chicken into bite sized pieces. Toss in large bowl with flour. In 12" skillet over medium high heat, cook chicken in a little oil (or Pam cooking spray). Cook half the chicken at a time until tender and browned, removing from pan when done. Cover and keep warm. In blender or food processor, place onion, yogurt, lemon juice, salt (optional), sugar, all spices and 3 tablespoons oil. Cover and blend until puréed. Pour into 12" skillet and heat over medium heat to boiling, stirring occasionally. Reduce heat to low. Keep warm. Add chicken to sauce and toss to coat pieces well. Serve with rice.

Serves 6   Beth DeWolfe

Curried Maple Chicken

Down east meets East! Sweetly exotic!

4	tablespoons peanut oil
1	tablespoon fresh ginger root, sliced
1	pound chicken breast, boned and skinned, cut in strips
½	cup flour
2	cloves garlic, minced
1	sweet red pepper, diced
	Juice of 4 limes
½	cup unsalted peanuts
¼	cup coconut
¼	cup maple syrup
2	tablespoons curry powder
¾	cup vanilla flavored yogurt
	Pinch cayenne pepper

Heat oil in skillet or wok over medium-high heat. Add ginger root and cook until golden. Remove. Dredge chicken in flour and add to oil. Sauté 3 minutes, stirring with wooden spoon. Add garlic and red pepper. Cook 1 minute longer. Remove from skillet. Squeeze lime juice over chicken. Cool. Mix remaining ingredients together. Add to cooled chicken. Chill 30 minutes. Serve over lettuce greens, as complement to rice.

Serves 2 to 4   Karen Pulkkinen and Leland Faulkner
                                               Performing Artists

Seal Rock Chicken

Makes its own sauce. Will multiply. May make ahead and reheat at 350 degrees for 15 minutes or until hot.

1	broiler, cut up
	Salt and pepper to taste
	Paprika
1	onion, sliced
3	to 4 tomatoes, sliced (unpeeled)

1½ pounds zucchini, sliced
(unpeeled)
½ to 1 teaspoon oregano
½ to 1 teaspoon basil
Garlic powder, a few shakes
Parsley, add before serving

Sprinkle chicken with paprika, salt and pepper. Brown 10 minutes and place in casserole. Add onion, tomatoes, salt, pepper and herbs. Do not add liquid. Cover and bake at 350 degrees for 15-20 minutes. Then add zucchini. Bake 15 minutes longer or until zucchini is cooked.

Serves 4   Peggy Ross

Marinated Arti-Chicken Bake

This recipe is a great favorite at the Blaine House. It is easy to serve and especially good for buffets. Easy to double or triple for larger groups.

2 pounds chicken cutlets
Milk
Seasoned bread crumbs
Cooking oil
2 jars marinated artichokes
(6 ounces each)
1 pound mushrooms, sliced
¼ cup tarragon vinegar

Preheat oven to 350 degrees

Cut chicken into 2 inch strips. Dip each piece in milk. Coat each piece with crumbs. Fry in oil and set aside. Empty one jar of artichokes and liquid into baking pan. Cover with ½ of mushrooms. Place chicken on top. Cover with remaining mushrooms and artichokes. Pour tarragon vinegar over. Cover. Bake 45 minutes at 350 degrees.

Serves 6   John McKernan, Jr.
                                               Governor, State of Maine

Maine Maple Chicken

Each year when the sap begins to flow I recall the sweet scents from my grandmother's kitchen when she would make her marvelous maple chicken. No Maine cookbook would be complete without a recipe using maple syrup. This one is cherished by me, by my family and by anyone else who has tried it.

5	chicken breast quarters
1	large onion
5	ounces tomato paste
2	tablespoons Dijon mustard
¼	cup olive or vegetable oil
½	cup dark maple syrup
¼	cup white vinegar
½	cup water
	Salt and fresh ground pepper (optional)

Preheat oven to 375 degrees

Combine all ingredients except chicken, onion and water in a large mixing bowl. Whisk well. Set sauce aside. Place chicken pieces in casserole dish. Peel and slice onion and tuck between chicken pieces. Add water to bottom of casserole. Bake at 375 degrees for 30 minutes. Remove from oven. Ladle sauce over chicken pieces. Return to oven for 20 minutes. Baste frequently. Garnish with a sprig of fresh parsley.

Serves 4 to 5   Brenda Curley

Chicken Dijon

6	to 8 boneless chicken pieces
3	to 4 tablespoons butter
1	minced onion
½	cup white wine
1	cup half and half cream
2	tablespoons Dijon-style mustard
	Dash of pepper

Preheat oven to 350 degrees

Cut chicken into serving size pieces and sauté in butter. Lower flame. Cook 10 minutes until done. Remove chicken to shallow baking dish. Cook onions until tender. Add wine. Let simmer to reduce alcohol. With wire whisk, stir in cream and mustard. Pour over chicken. May be served immediately or prepared ahead and warmed in 350 degree oven for 20 minutes.

Serves 6 to 8   Nancy Richardson

Chicken Diana

4   whole chicken breasts
1   cup flour
1   teaspoon baking powder
1¼ tablespoons and ½ teaspoon cornstarch
1⅓ cups and ½ cup water
½   cup orange juice
½   cup vinegar
½   cup sugar
1   can mandarin oranges, drained
2   tablespoons oil
2   tablespoons margarine

Batter: mix 1 cup flour, 1 teaspoon baking powder, ½ teaspoon cornstarch and 1⅓ cups water and let stand one hour.

Sauce: bring to boil ½ cup orange juice, ½ cup vinegar, and ½ cup sugar. Add 1¼ tablespoons cornstarch diluted in ½ cup cold water. Stir until thickened and add 1 can mandarin oranges, drained.

Chicken: dip pounded boneless chicken breasts in batter. Sauté in mixture of 2 tablespoons oil and 2 tablespoons margarine. Serve on rice with sauce over all.

Serves 4   Mary Haggerty
                          Lincoln House Country Inn, Dennysville

Marinated Boneless Chicken Breasts

This is a very easy recipe that's best if cooked out on the grill.

3 to 4 boneless chicken breasts, halved
½ cup vegetable oil (preferably peanut)
½ cup soy sauce
2 tablespoons white vinegar
2 cloves garlic, diced
1 teaspoon grated fresh ginger root
1 to 2 scallions, chopped

Arrange chicken breasts in single layer in shallow dish (for marinating). In a small bowl, combine the oil, soy sauce, vinegar, garlic, ginger root and scallions. Pour this mix over the chicken breasts. Cover and refrigerate to marinate for at least 6 hours, turning the breasts over every 2-3 hours. Grill or broil approximately 5 minutes on each side. The remaining marinade can be saved and heated to boiling to serve over the cooked chicken and is wonderful on a side serving of rice.

Serves 4 to 6   Lisa Barron

Chicken Chèvre Pâtisserie

This is an easy dish to make ahead of time and place in the oven, just 35 minutes before serving.

4 boneless, skinless breasts of chicken
6 ounces soft goat cheese
1 teaspoon fresh or ½ teaspoon dried basil
1 teaspoon fresh or ½ teaspoon dried thyme
1 clove garlic, finely minced
Salt and pepper to taste

Puff pastry sheets (can be
bought frozen at the
supermarket)
1   egg, beaten with a splash of
water and touch of salt

Preheat oven to 425 degrees

Defrost puff pastry sheets. Cut into 5 inch squares and place on lightly
floured surface. Mix the goat cheese, herbs and garlic together. Lay out
the breasts of chicken and pat dry. Take 1 heaping tablespoon of cheese
mixture and place in center of breast but over thicker portion. Roll thin
end of breast over cheese. Lift breast gently into center of a square of
puff pastry. Brush the outer edges of the pastry square with the egg
wash. This will act as a sealant. Bring the points of the puff pastry square
together so that they overlap each other and the chicken is completely
enveloped within the pastry. Gently turn the enclosed chicken breast
over, placing it on a well oiled heavy cookie sheet or parchment paper
on a cookie sheet. Brush the puff pastry with egg wash and, with a scrap
of dough, cut out a decoration and place on top of the completed
chicken breast. Egg wash the decoration. Before baking, take a skewer
or rounded sharp object and pierce the top of the dough to allow the
steam to escape during baking. (Do this after you have egg washed the
item, otherwise the hole will be closed by the egg wash). Place the
decorated chicken breasts on the center shelf in the preheated oven to
bake for 25 minutes. When browned and done, remove from the oven
and let cool for 10 minutes before serving. Note: check the color of the
puff pastry after 20 minutes and if it has not darkened to your liking,
move to the top shelf in the oven for the last five minutes.

Serves 4   James D. Wall, Chef
                                            Squire Tarbox Inn, Wiscasset

Serve hot curried fruit with chicken. Combine
apricots, pineapple chunks, peaches or prunes with
some juice, butter and curry to taste.

Chicken Livers with Wine

½   pound chicken livers
2   tablespoons butter
2   tablespoons chopped onion
¼   pound mushrooms, sliced
2   tablespoons flour
½   cup strong chicken stock
½   cup good white wine
½   teaspoon chopped thyme
½   teaspoon chopped parsley

Cut and trim livers. Melt butter, sauté chopped onions and sliced mushrooms. Add chicken livers and sauté for 3 minutes. Stir in flour. Add chicken stock and wine, stir until smooth. Add herbs and simmer 10 minutes, stirring occasionally. Salt and pepper to taste. Serve on toast or hot rice.

Serves 2   Mrs. Horace W. Peters

Turkey Meatballs

This recipe was adapted from my mother's Christmas meatball recipe which was made with 1½ pounds of hamburg and ½ pound hot sausage meat.

2   pounds ground turkey
½   cup Romano cheese
¾   cup Italian flavored bread crumbs
⅓   cups raisins
⅓   cup pinenuts
2   eggs
½   cup milk
4   cloves garlic, pressed
½   teaspoon ground pepper
1   tablespoon parsley and sweet basil
1   teaspoon chervil
1   teaspoon savory
2   teaspoons oregano

Mix all ingredients in a large bowl. Form into balls and sauté in olive oil on all sides for 15 minutes. Remove meatballs. Place on paper towels. Add to your favorite spaghetti sauce.

Makes 20 to 30 meatballs   Mary Ann Hughes

Milbridge Colonial Pie

Almost more popular than the turkey event that precedes it. Simple post-holiday supper. Serve with mixed green salad and vinaigrette dressing.

2   cups whole kernel corn
1   tablespoon chopped parsley
   (fresh or dried)
⅓   cup evaporated milk
2   eggs, separated
1   12-ounce package corn muffin
   mix
1   tablespoon chopped pimento
1½ teaspoons onion salt
3   to 4 drops Tabasco
   Sliced or diced cooked turkey to
   cover bottom of baking dish
2   to 3 pimentos for garnish
1½ cups left over gravy

Preheat oven to 350 degrees

Combine all ingredients except egg whites and turkey in mixing bowl. Stir. Batter should be lumpy. Gently fold in stiffly beaten egg whites. Place generous layer of turkey in shallow baking dish. Pour on gravy and spoon in batter topping. Bake in 350 degree oven for 1 hour. Cut "poinsettia" petals from whole pimentos for garnish and serve.

Serves 5 to 6   D. Lombard Brett

Turkey Muddle

Prepare ahead of time except for parsley. Serve in casserole or chafing dish.

5	cups chopped cooked turkey or chicken
1	green pepper, finely chopped
1	red pepper, finely chopped
1	medium onion, finely chopped
¾	stick unsalted butter
¾	cup chicken stock
½	cup flour
¾	cup dry sherry
½	cup half and half
1½	cups diced cooked potato
1	tablespoon Worcestershire sauce
½	cup minced fresh parsley

In large iron skillet sauté peppers and onions in butter until tender. Add flour and stir for 3 minutes. Forms roux. Add sherry, chicken stock and half and half. Whisk thoroughly and bring to boil. Stir in remaining ingredients. Add salt and pepper to taste. Cook for 15 minutes on medium heat. Stir occasionally. Thin, if too thick, with half and half.

Serves 8

Taccino Tonnata

1	7-ounce can white meat tuna, drained
4	to 6 anchovy fillets
1	large clove garlic
½	teaspoon dried basil
¾	cup mayonnaise
1	tablespoon lemon juice
½	cup olive oil
1¼	to 1½ pounds roast turkey breast, rolled and thinly sliced
1	heaping tablespoon capers Freshly ground pepper to taste

Place tuna, anchovy, garlic, basil, mayonnaise and lemon juice in food processor. Purée about 20 seconds. While machine is on, pour in oil slowly. Consistency should be smooth. Check seasoning. Add freshly ground pepper. Arrange sliced turkey on lettuce on serving platter and spoon sauce around border of turkey. Sprinkle turkey with capers and serve immediately. Garnish with parsley and lemon wedges.

Serves 4   Marguerite Rafter

Spring House Stifado

Serve with good French bread, salad and lots of hearty red wine.

¼   cup butter
3   pounds chuck beef, cut into
     2" cubes
2   cups red wine
2   cups brown stock
6   ounce can tomato paste
¼   cup red wine vinegar
2   tablespoons light brown sugar
1½ teaspoons cumin
1   teaspoon minced garlic
½   teaspoon ground allspice
1   bay leaf
     Salt and pepper
18 small white onions which have
     been blanched, drained and
     peeled (frozen are o.k.)
½   pound mushrooms sautéed in
     3 tablespoons butter

In heavy kettle, melt ¼ cup butter, add cubed beef and toss to coat, do not brown. Add red wine, stock, tomato paste, red wine vinegar, brown sugar, cumin, garlic, allspice, bay leaf and salt and pepper. Bring to a boil and simmer for 1½ hours. Then add onions and simmer, covered, for 30 minutes. Add mushrooms. Remove bay leaf and serve in casserole.

Serves 6 to 8   Betsy Hunt and Peter Ralston

Tournados of Beef, Wild Mushroom Madeira Sauce

2 filets of beef tenderloin, 8-ounce
½ tablespoon olive oil
½ tablespoon butter
½ tablespoon garlic, minced with salt
¼ cup brandy
¼ cup Madeira
⅛ cup all purpose flour
4 crimea mushrooms (chanterelle) and
4 shiitake mushrooms or,
6 ounces cultivated, farm-raised wild mushrooms

Sauté tenderloin in olive oil/butter. Cook to desired temperature (medium rare, medium, etc.). Remove from pan. Add garlic, mushrooms and liquor. Reduce and dust with flour. Cook thoroughly and put tenderloin back into pan. Serve with green vegetable, fresh salad and new potatoes.

Serves 2   Louis Kiefer, Chef
                                    Asticou Inn, Northeast Harbor

Company Casserole

Great buffet dish.

2 cups raw wild rice
4 cups water
2 teaspoons salt (I use less, or omit)
2 pounds ground beef
1 pound fresh mushrooms, sliced
½ cup chopped celery
1 cup chopped onion
½ cup butter
½ cup sliced water chestnuts
¼ cup chopped black olives
¼ cup soy sauce
2 cups sour cream

2   teaspoons salt
¼   teaspoon pepper
½   cup slivered almonds
    Parsley sprigs for garnish

Preheat oven to 350 degrees

Wash wild rice. In covered pan, gently cook wild rice in water with salt for 45 minutes. Drain rice. Brown ground beef and set aside. Sauté mushrooms, celery and onion in butter for 5 minutes. Combine soy sauce, sour cream, salt and pepper. Add cooked wild rice, beef, onion, mushrooms, celery and olives. Add almonds (saving a few for garnish). Place mixture in a lightly greased 3-quart casserole. Bake at 350 degrees for 1 hour, uncovered. Add water, if needed, and season to taste. Stir several times. Garnish with reserved almonds and parsley.

Serves 12   Mrs. Richard C. Britton

Flambéed Pepper Steak

4   beef tenderloin steaks
1   small onion, chopped
4   teaspoons black or green
    peppercorns, crushed well
1   tablespoon butter or margarine
1   teaspoon salt
3   to 4 tablespoons beef consommé
⅔   cup whipping cream
3   tablespoons brandy

Combine chopped onion and crushed peppercorns. Press peppercorn mixture into both sides of steak. Heat butter until lightly browned in skillet. Add steaks. Brown well on one side and turn over. Brown on other side. Add salt. Remove steaks to dish and keep warm. Add cream to pan. Stir and cook until reduced. Once reduced, add beef consommé. Strain and save cream mixture. Rinse pan. Heat skillet and add steaks. Pour brandy over steaks and ignite. Add cream mixture and let cook for about 2 minutes.

Serves 4   Greg Welch
                                                    Artist

Grilled Steak with Lime Marinade

⅓ cup fresh lime juice
(about 3 medium limes)
¼ cup salad oil
¼ cup molasses
2 tablespoons mustard
1 teaspoon grated lime peel
1 teaspoon garlic powder
½ teaspoon pepper
½ teaspoon salt
2 pounds top round or top sirloin

Mix all ingredients with a whisk. Place steak in a clear plastic bag, set in a deep pan. Pour marinade over steak and seal bag. Refrigerate 4-8 hours, turning bag several times. Bring steak to room temperature before cooking. Grill steak over medium heat until done to your preference. Use tongs or a wide spatula to turn meat on the grill (forks pierce the meat and allow the flavorful juices to drain away). To serve, slice thinly on the diagonal.

Serves 4 to 6   Nonie Pierce

Meatloaf

1 to 2 tablespoons olive oil
1 cup diced onion
½ cup diced celery
2 minced garlic cloves
1 teaspoon basil
1 teaspoon oregano
2 teaspoons thyme
1½ pounds ground beef
¾ pound sweet Italian sausage,
casings removed
½ cup chopped sun-dried tomatoes
½ cup minced Italian parsley
2 beaten eggs
½ cup fine dry bread crumbs
1 teaspoon salt
1 teaspoon pepper

Preheat oven to 350 degrees

Put olive oil in skillet and sauté onions, celery, garlic, basil, oregano and thyme until tender, about 15 minutes. In large bowl, combine ground beef, sausage and sautéed vegetables. Stir in the tomatoes, parsley, eggs, crumbs, salt and pepper. Mix thoroughly with hands. Form into 2 loaves and place in large shallow baking dish. Bake 1 hour or a little more, occasionally pouring off the juices.

Serves 4 to 6   Sheila Donaldson

Bahamian Butterflied Lamb

A savory way to do lamb.

1   whole leg of lamb, boned and butterflied
½   to ¾ cup olive oil
2   lemons, squeezed
1   teaspoon salt
½   teaspoon oregano
2   to 3 large garlic cloves
2   cans peach halves
1   jar mint jelly
    Nutmeg or cinnamon
    (a sprinkle)

Preheat oven to broil

Coat lamb with olive oil. Squeeze lemon over lamb, both sides. Put crushed garlic, salt, cracked pepper and oregano on both sides and marinate 2-3 hours. To cook, put lamb under broiler, turning to give a good crust on both sides. Do this about 5 minutes to a side. Turn oven to 325 degrees and cook for 40-45 minutes. Serve cooked lamb with peach halves which have been dotted with butter and 1 teaspoon of mint jelly and run under the broiler until lightly browned.

Serves 10   Alice H. Rand
                                                      Trustee

Lamb Louise

May be partially prepared several hours before serving.

Lamb:
1 boned leg of lamb (reserve bones)
¼ pound butter
1 teaspoon garlic powder
1 teaspoon salt
1 teaspoon cayenne
Fresh parsley

Preheat oven to 375 degrees.

Lamb: remove all fat. Cream together butter, garlic powder, salt, pepper and cover roast with this mixture. On double thickness foil, place bones with roast on top. Wrap tightly and refrigerate overnight. Remove 2 hours before roasting and roast (wrapped) at 375 degrees for 35 minutes (medium) or 45 minutes (well done). When done, remove from oven, unwrap, and strain juices into a saucepan. (May be prepared up to this point ahead of time.) Turn oven up to 400 degrees, discard bones, place roast in open foil and return to oven for 30 minutes.

Gravy:
½ pint sour cream
¾ teaspoon saffron (optional)
1 teaspoon cornstarch
¾ to 1 bottle capers
Paprika

Gravy: add sour cream to juices and saffron (if used). Bring to boil. Mix cornstarch with 3 teaspoons cold water, add to gravy and boil 4 minutes. Add capers and cook 1 minute more. Keep warm (covered). When ready to serve, slice lamb and arrange on serving platter. Sprinkle with chopped parsley and serve gravy separately.

Serves 6 to 8   Tinker Barron

Chadbourn's Marvelous Marinade for Pork

One of the best marinades for pork and can be used for chicken, lamb or beef kabobs equally well.

Marinade:
½ cup Kikkoman soy sauce
2 cloves garlic, minced
⅓ cup vegetable oil
⅓ cup lemon juice
1 tablespoon curry powder
1 tablespoon chili powder
3 tablespoons honey
1 large onion, finely chopped
Pork:
8 boneless center pork chops or pork fillets cut into 1½" cubes
8 small light green Italian peppers
16 medium small white onions, parboiled for 5 minutes

Marinate meat for 3 to 4 hours in large bowl. Arrange 5 pieces of pork cubes on skewer. Arrange separate skewers of halved peppers and onions. Broil over hot coals for about 20 minutes, until pork is well browned and vegetables are brown. Spoon some of the marinade over meat. Serve with couscous or wheat pilaf.

Serves 6 to 8   Alfred C. Chadbourn
                                                          Artist

*Venison is an unbelievable
substitute for beef in Boeuf Bourguignon.*

Prune (or Apricot) Stuffed Pork Tenderloin

This is easy, delicious and good cold if there's any left over. Wild rice is nice with this.

1	package pork tenderloin (2 pieces)
1	box pitted prunes or 1 bag dried apricots
	Apple cider or cranberry juice or wine or broth

Preheat oven to 350 degrees

Place meat on flat surface. Slit gently 2 or 3 times (not through—only to flatten). Put a line of prunes or apricots the length of the meat, cover with other piece. Tie 4 or 5 times to keep the two together. Brown in a little oil or butter or margarine in skillet. Transfer to casserole. Pour 1½ cups liquid over, cover tightly with foil and cook 40 minutes in 350 degree oven. Remove string, then slice and serve with liquid over or in gravy boat.

Serves 4 to 6   Phyllis R. Chandler

Pork in Cider

6	pound loin of pork, boned and rolled
2½	teaspoons salt
¾	teaspoon freshly ground black pepper
8	large apples, cored
8	large onions, peeled
1½	cups cider
2	tablespoons flour or cornstarch
¼	cup cognac

Preheat oven to 375 degrees.

Rub pork with salt and pepper and roast for 1½ hours. Pour off fat and arrange apples and onions around pork. Add 1 cup cider, reduce heat to

325 degrees and roast 1¼ hours longer, basting frequently. Remove strings from pork and arrange on a hot serving platter with apples and onions. Skim fat from gravy, place pan over low heat and stir in flour to thicken. Gradually add the rest of the cider and the cognac, stirring constantly. Simmer for 5 minutes and serve in a gravy boat.

Serves 8   Susan Donnell Konkel
                                                                  Trustee

Tourtière (Pork Pie)

This is a traditional French Canadian midnight supper on Christmas Eve, served after church.

1½ pounds ground pork
4   to 6 potatoes, cubed
1   medium sized onion
4   celery stalks, with leaves
4   whole cloves
4   tablespoons Bell seasoning
     Salt and pepper to taste
     Pie crust (top and bottom)

Preheat oven to 350 degrees

Cook pork in skillet. Drain fat. Boil potatoes with the onion, celery and cloves. When potatoes are tender, drain water and remove onion, celery and cloves. Mash potato slightly, leaving small chunks. Put Bell seasoning, salt and pepper in cooked pork. Combine seasoned pork and potatoes, and put mixture into pie crust bottom. Cover with pie crust top, brush top with milk, and put in preheated 350 degree oven for 45 minutes or until crust is golden.

Serves 4 to 6   Denise Lord

Pork Chops and Rice

Uses only one pot; clean up is a snap. Delicious flavor combination, a family favorite. Great for mother when she needs to pick up a child or run an errand near dinner hour. Presto, a meal!

6   pork chops (¾"-1" thick)
½   cup uncooked rice
3¾ cups strained tomatoes
3   tablespoons chopped fresh green pepper
3   tablespoons chopped onion
2   teaspoons salt
¼   teaspoon pepper
2   tablespoons olive oil

Heat oil in a 10" skillet or Dutch pot. Brown chops on both sides. Combine all other ingredients. Pour over chops. Place lid on Dutch pot. Cook over medium heat until steaming. Switch to simmer. Cook 60 minutes. Do not remove lid. Remove from skillet or Dutch pot to serving platter.

Serves 6   Ann L. Walz

Grilled Pork with Rosemary

We like to serve this with white Texmati or Basmati rice. If you are using dry rosemary, try putting it in the wine and microwaving (gently warming). It will bring out the flavor and aroma of the rosemary.

2   pounds lean pork, cut in cubes
1   cup dry white wine
1   tablespoon minced garlic
1   tablespoon rosemary leaves, fresh (or 1 teaspoon dry)
2   tablespoons minced parsley
1   teaspoon grated lemon rind
    Salt and pepper
2   tablespoons olive oil
2   tablespoons wine vinegar

> 2 tablespoons melted butter, optional

Blend all and marinate 2-4 hours. Skewer and grill, don't overcook! Remove from skewers and drizzle with melted butter, if desired.

Serves 4

Broiled Veal Chops

This recipe would work well with ¾" thick veal steak or cutlets.

Chops:
6 1-inch thick rib or loin veal chops
10 to 12 ounces mushrooms cut in slices about ¼" thick
3 tablespoons finely chopped shallots (or green onion)
3 ounces vermouth
¼ cup beef bouillon
Cooking oil

Paste:
½ stick butter
½ cup bread crumbs
½ teaspoon basil
½ teaspoon oregano
1 tablespoon finely chopped shallots (in addition to above)

Prepare paste by combining all ingredients in a bowl to a consistency that allows you to form a paste. Place paste in refrigerator. Salt and pepper the chops. Brown the chops in oil about six minutes on each side. Arrange the chops in a pan. Spread the paste to cover each chop. Scatter shallots and mushrooms around the chops. Pour in vermouth and bouillon. Place in hot oven (450 degrees) for 12 minutes. Then place 4" to 6" under broiler for 8 minutes, taking care not to burn the topping which should be a crusty brown.

Serves 6   Robert Edmondson

Chargrilled Veal Chops with Apple Fritters and An Apple Brandy Sauce

4   14-ounce veal loin chops
2   Granny Smith apples, peeled, cored and thinly sliced
1   cup flour
⅓   cup sugar
½   tablespoon baking powder
1   teaspoon salt
1   egg
⅓   cup milk
2   tablespoons melted butter

Fritters: sift the dry ingredients into a bowl and stir in the remaining ingredients. Add the apples. Fry in small batches until crispy. Keep warm.

Apple Brandy Sauce:
2   shallots, minced
1   apple, minced
6   mushrooms, chopped
½   cup white wine
1   cup cider
1   cup veal stock
½   cup heavy cream
¼   cup apple brandy
    Salt and pepper

Apple Brandy Sauce: sweat the shallots, apple and mushrooms in a small saucepan. Deglaze the pan with the white wine. Add the cider and reduce the sauce by half. Add the veal stock and reduce again by half. Add the heavy cream and reduce the sauce until it has slightly thickened. Add the brandy, salt and pepper. Strain through a sieve and adjust seasonings. Keep warm.

To assemble: grill the veal chops to desired doneness. Put a little sauce in the middle of a warm plate and top with a veal chop. Arrange the fritters and your choice of vegetables around the veal and serve.

Serves 4

Edward Gannon
The White Barn Inn, Kennebunkport

Veal Rib Chops with Sundried Tomatoes & Basil

Veal:

4	veal rib chops, 8-10 ounces each
1	tablespoon canola oil
2	tablespoons unsalted butter
1	chopped shallot
1	clove chopped garlic
¼	cup butter
	Salt and pepper to taste

Sauce:

2	tablespoons glacé de viande
½	cup heavy cream
1	heaping tablespoon chopped sundried tomatoes
1	tablespoon fresh basil
2	ounces dry white wine

Preheat oven to 400 degrees

Season chops with salt and pepper. With burner on high, heat oil in skillet with 1 tablespoon butter until butter stops sizzling. Then immediately place chops in skillet, shaking pan to keep from sticking. Allow to brown — about 1 minute — then turn and brown chops on the other side 1-2 minutes. Place skillet in preheated oven to finish cooking chops, 5 to 10 minutes, depending upon thickness of chops. They should be pink in the center. Place chops on a warm platter and keep warm while you finish the sauce. Pour off any oil remaining in the pan. Add the chopped shallot and garlic and sauté for 1 minute. Add the white wine and sundried tomatoes and reduce until most of the wine has evaporated and what remains in the pan forms a thick glaze. Add the heavy cream and glacé de viande and boil for 1 minute. Add the basil and butter and swirl the pan until the butter has melted. Taste and adjust seasonings as necessary. Pour sauce over chops and serve.

Serves 4

Daniel F. Gore, Chef
Cumberland Club, Portland

Veal and Mushroom Stew

Fine without a starch but can be served with a side dish of linguine. Preparation time: forever, but worth it!

12 tablespoons unsalted butter
3 pounds veal, cut into 1" cubes
7½ tablespoons flour
3 teaspoons paprika
2¼ teaspoons coriander
Salt and pepper to taste
4½ cups plum tomatoes, seeded and diced
3 cups chicken broth
2¼ cups yellow onions, cut into slivers
18 large whole shallots, peeled
3 cloves garlic
½ cup chopped parsley, plus some for garnish
1½ tablespoons dried tarragon
Grated zest of 1½ oranges
¾ pound white mushrooms, cut in half lengthwise
¾ cup heavy cream

Preheat oven to 350 degrees

Melt 6 tablespoons of butter in heavy flameproof casserole. Add veal and cook, turning frequently (do not brown) over low heat. Stir together 3 tablespoons flour, paprika, coriander, salt and pepper, and sprinkle this over veal. Cook over low heat, stirring, for another 5 minutes (do not let veal brown). Add 3 cups diced tomatoes, broth, onions, shallots, garlic, ½ cup parsley, tarragon and orange zest. Bring to boil on stove. Cover and bake in oven for 1¼ hours until veal is tender. While stew is baking, melt 3 tablespoons butter in skillet. Quickly sauté mushroom halves. Reserve. Remove stew from oven and pour it through strainer over a bowl. Reserve stew and cooking liquid separately (can be made a day ahead to this point). Return casserole to medium heat on top of stove and melt remaining 4½ tablespoons butter in it. Sprinkle in remaining 4½ tablespoons flour, whisk constantly over low heat for 3 minutes.

Whisk reserved cooking liquid slowly into butter and flour mixture. Simmer and stir for 5 minutes. Whisk in cream and season to taste. Return veal stew to casserole. Stir in remaining 1½ cups tomatoes and reserved mushrooms. Simmer to heat through. Transfer to serving dish and sprinkle with parsley.

Serves 6 to 8   Jack Evans
                                                                  Trustee

Veal Dijon

½   pound sliced mushrooms
6   tablespoons unsalted butter
2   tablespoons chopped shallots
4   veal scallops, 5-6 ounces each,
    pounded
    Salt and pepper
1   cup heavy cream
1½ tablespoons Dijon mustard
2   tablespoons lemon juice

Heat 2 tablespoons unsalted butter in medium skillet. Add mushrooms and shallots and sauté over moderately high heat just until limp. Remove from pan and reserve. Heat 2 tablespoons unsalted butter in the same skillet. Sauté veal scallops, two at a time, adding more butter as needed, for not more than a minute on each side. Transfer to warm plate and sprinkle with salt and pepper. In a small bowl, whisk together cream and mustard. Pour mixture into hot skillet and cook over high heat, scraping up brown bits on bottom of pan, until sauce is reduced by half. Add lemon juice and mix. Return veal and mushrooms and all liquid to pan just long enough to coat with sauce and heat through. Serve with rice on the side, never under the veal.

Serves 4   Mary Haggerty
                                           Lincoln House, Dennysville

Either pork or chicken is an
excellent substitute for veal.

Veal Jayscott

J. Scott Smart (1902-1960), my husband, was known best for his starring role as "The Fat Man" of radio. He was a screen actor, recording artist, a jazz musician, painter and amateur chef. This is one of his favorites.

1   pound veal
½   pint sour cream
¼   cup olive oil
1   large garlic clove
¼   pound mushrooms, sliced
2   ounces sherry
    Chopped chives

Cut the veal into 3" thin squares and dredge in flour. Heat the olive oil. Chop garlic. Add mushrooms and brown in the oil. Brown the veal quickly. Add seasoning to taste and then the sherry. Reduce the heat for 3 minutes. Add sour cream and serve with chopped chives.

Serves 3 to 4   Mary-Leigh Smart
                                                          Artist

Saddle of Venison with Buckwheat Cakes and Juniper Sauce

Venison:

1½ pound boneless venison loin, trimmed of silver membranes
2   ounces fresh Moulard or Barbary duck foie gras (or substitute good quality canned foie gras; do not sear, but purée directly with sauce ingredients)
1   teaspoon fresh ginger root, finely minced
6   juniper berries, crushed
    Salt and fresh milled black pepper to taste
2   medium shallots, peeled and minced

12 ounces rich brown stock (or
    substitute good quality canned
    beef consommé)
¼   cup heavy cream
¼   cup Armagnac or Cognac brandy
2   tablespoons olive oil
Buckwheat cakes:
1   tablespoon olive oil
1   egg
¼   cup all purpose flour
¼   cup buckwheat flour
½   cup buttermilk
1   teaspoon baking powder
    Pinch salt

Buckwheat cakes: beat egg with olive oil. Combine dry ingredients and add to egg mixture. Add enough buttermilk to make light batter. Cook on preheated griddle in two inch pancakes. Cook about 2 minutes on a side, turning once.

Venison: divide the venison loin into four equal portions and season with salt and pepper to taste. Heat a non-corroding skillet large enough to hold all four portions. Add the olive oil, heat until nearly smoking and add the venison. Over high heat, sear all surfaces of the meat. Remove to an ovenproof platter, and reserve. Pour off the excess olive oil. Sear the foie gras in the pan, cooking for thirty to forty seconds on each side over moderate heat. Drain the foie gras on absorbent paper and place in blender jar. Pour off excess fat from skillet. Add the stock or consommé, stirring and scraping to dissolve any bits of caramelized meat juices. Add the minced shallots, minced ginger root and juniper berries. Boil to reduce to one cup. Add the cream. Boil to reduce to one cup. Add the Armagnac or Cognac. Bring to a boil, simmer one minute and add to foie gras in blender jar. Purée thirty seconds. Pour back into skillet. Adjust the seasoning with salt and milled pepper to taste, and reserve. Cook the venison in 350 degree oven for five to seven minutes, or until it registers an internal temperature of 130 degrees (medium rare) or to desired temperature. Slice the portions across their length into four slices each and arrange on four dinner plates. Spoon the sauce around and arrange the buckwheat cakes alongside the slices.

Serves 4   Sam Hayward, Chef and Food Manager
                                    Harraseeket Inn, Freeport

Whole Split Pheasant

Absolutely delicious and needs only seasoning of salt and pepper to taste.

1	pheasant, cleaned and split
4	tablespoons butter
1	cup half and half cream
	Parsley for garnish

Preheat oven to 250 degrees

Place four tablespoons of butter in casserole, add pheasant, breast side down. Sauté over medium heat until light brown. Turn pheasant in casserole (breast side up), pour cream over and put in 250 degree oven. Cook for 30 to 45 minutes. Garnish with parsley.

Serves 2   Mr. & Mrs. William Tudor Gardiner

Sausage Pie

A favorite of young painters in Greenwich Village in the '50s, this recipe has been passed along through the art world for nearly a half century and became a specialty of the Perkins Cove art colony in Ogunquit.

1	2-pound coil sweet sausage
	White pepper
	Pinch of nutmeg
	Mozzarella cheese
	White wine
	Olive oil
	Mustard

Fresh sausage from an Italian pork store is preferred (Munjoy Hill in Portland or the North End in Boston). Purchase a two-pound coil of sweet sausage not yet made into links. Place coil in frying pan (one with a metal handle is best). Just cover with a good white wine. Add pepper and a pinch or two of nutmeg. Poach for 20 minutes. Remove wine from pan, holding sausage with cover. Return to low flame and add enough olive oil to cover bottom of pan. Fry for 10+ minutes. While it is frying, cut a ball of mozzarella in half-inch slices, coating one side with mustard.

Light the broiler and turn to high flame. Place cheese, mustard side down on sausage. Broil until cheese melts and starts to brown. Remove. Serve immediately, cut like a pie.

Serves 4   Helen C. Horn

Sausage and Egg Casserole

A great brunch recipe.

1   pound bulk sausage
½   pound grated sharp Cheddar
½   teaspoon dry mustard
½   teaspoon paprika
1   cup sour cream
10 to 16 eggs (depending on crowd)
    Greek seasoning (available at
    food speciality shops), optional

Preheat oven to 325 degrees

Cook and drain sausage. Mix sour cream with spices and ½ of the cheese. Spray 2 or 3 quart baking dish with vegetable spray. Spread sausage mixture on bottom of dish (this can be done the day before). Beat eggs and pour over sausage mixture. Top with remaining ½ cheese. Sprinkle with Greek seasoning. Bake at 325 degrees for 40-45 minutes or until eggs are set.

Serves 8 to 14   Mary Haggerty
                                  Lincoln House Country Inn, Dennysville

*One half egg is 2 tablespoons
of 1 beaten egg.*

Calves Liver in Mustard and Vinegar Sauce

¾ cup whipping cream
1 tablespoon Dijon mustard
2 tablespoons fresh, or
1 tablespoon dried, tarragon
½ teaspoon salt
¼ teaspoon pepper
2 pounds calves liver, cut in
1" slices
2 tablespoons unsalted butter
1 tablespoon olive oil
Salt and pepper
1 tablespoon unsalted butter
4 cups thinly sliced onions
½ teaspoon thyme
¼ cup white wine vinegar
1 tablespoon unsalted butter
1 tablespoon flour
Snipped fresh parsley

Combine cream, mustard, tarragon, salt and pepper in a small bowl. Reserve. Sauté liver in 2 tablespoons butter and 1 tablespoon oil until light brown (liver should be rare), about 2 minutes. Season to taste. Remove from pan. Add 1 tablespoon butter to pan drippings. Stir in onions and thyme. Sauté, stirring frequently until brown. Reduce heat to low and simmer, covered, until onions are soft, about 10 minutes. Stir in vinegar. Increase heat to high and boil uncovered until vinegar evaporates. Stir in reserved cream mixture. Heat to boiling. Cook until slightly thickened, 3-5 minutes. Mix 1 tablespoon butter and 1 tablespoon flour on a small plate. Whisk into onion mixture gradually, whisking until smooth. Taste and adjust seasonings. Return liver to skillet. Reduce heat to low and heat thoroughly, stirring gently. Arrange on serving platter and garnish with parsley.

Serves 6

Eileen Farrar
Trustee

Desserts

Copper Beech Tree

Andrew Wyeth's Birthday Meringue

6   egg whites (at room temperature)
½   teaspoon cream of tartar
    Dash of salt
2   cups superfine granulated sugar
½   teaspoon vanilla
½   teaspoon almond flavoring
½   pint heavy cream
1   cup macaroons
1   cup strawberries, chopped

Preheat oven to 275 degrees

Line a cookie sheet with parchment. In copper bowl beat egg whites with cream of tartar and salt until frothy. Very gradually add sugar until stiff (about 10 minutes). Beat in flavorings. Spoon meringue onto paper in a ring shape. Bake at 275 degrees for 1¼ hours. Turn oven off, leaving meringue in closed oven for 2 hours without opening door. One hour before serving, crumble 1 cup macaroons into ½ pint heavy cream until softened. Whip cream until stiff. Spread over meringue. Fill center with sweetened chopped strawberries. Does not hold over until next day.

Betsy Wyeth

Brown Sugar Tapioca

This recipe was made originally with molasses instead of brown sugar by my Grandmother Wilcox. My mother preferred brown sugar rather than stringy, sticky molasses, but the youngsters preferred the molasses.

1   cup brown sugar
2   tablespoons tapioca
2   cups boiling water

Put in double boiler. Cook 40 minutes, stir often. Serve with cream.

Serves 4

Rev. Dr. Richard F. Wilcox

Tiramisu

Translation: "Carry Me Up To Heaven."

5 cups strong coffee
32 ladyfingers
10 egg yolks
10 tablespoons sugar
1 pound mascarpone cheese
1 to 2 tablespoons Marsala
2 cups heavy cream
2 tablespoons unsweetened cocoa powder

Pour the cold coffee into a large pie plate. Dip ladyfingers very quickly into the coffee and line the bottom of a 12" x 9" x 2" oval dish with the ladyfingers. In a large mixing bowl whisk the eggs and sugar until frothy. Add the mascarpone and Marsala, whisk until well blended and smooth. In another bowl, whisk the cream until stiff and fold into the mascarpone mixture until well blended and smooth. Spoon and smooth about ½ of the mixture over the ladyfingers. Dip the remaining ladyfingers quickly into the coffee. Arrange another layer of ladyfingers over the cheese mixture and spoon and smooth the remaining mixture over the ladyfingers in an attractive design. Cover with plastic wrap and chill at least six hours. The Tiramisu can be frozen for up to two months. When ready to serve, sprinkle the cocoa powder through a fine sieve over the entire surface of the Tiramisu. Spoon portions onto individual plates.

Serves 8 to 10   Angela LeBlanc

Cold Lemon Soufflé

A handy do-ahead dessert.

1 tablespoon gelatin
¼ cup water
3 eggs, separated
1 cup sugar
1 lemon, grated rind and juice
2 cups heavy cream

Dissolve gelatin in water and melt over hot water. Beat egg yolks until light yellow. Add sugar and beat until smooth and pale. Add lemon juice and grated rind. Beat egg whites until stiff and fold into mixture. Beat cream and fold in. Place in a serving bowl. Chill for three hours.

Serves 6

Swedish Cream

2⅓ cups heavy cream
1   envelope gelatin
1   cup sugar
1   pint sour cream
1   teaspoon vanilla
2   to 3 cups berries or peaches
    (peeled and sliced)

Mix together 2⅓ cups heavy cream with 1 cup sugar and 1 envelope gelatin. Heat gently and stir until gelatin is completely dissolved. Cool until slightly thickened. Fold in 1 pint of sour cream and 1 teaspoon vanilla. Pour into mold. Chill in refrigerator until firm. Unmold and pour sweetened berries or peaches on top.

Serves 6 to 8   Alice Wallis

Coffee Soufflé with Marshmallows

Old fashioned and might have been forgotten.

24 regular marshmallows
1   cup strong hot coffee
1   pint heavy cream, whipped

Melt marshmallows in hot coffee. Cool. Fold in whipped cream. Pour into glass bowl or parfait glasses. Refrigerate several hours.

Serves 6   Zella B. Thomas

Traditional Spanish Custard

Fantastic!

2 cups lowfat milk
4 tablespoons brown sugar
2 eggs, beaten
⅓ cup sugar
½ teaspoon vanilla
¼ teaspoon salt

Preheat oven to 350 degrees

Press 1 tablespoon brown sugar into each of four custard cups. Beat eggs, sugar and salt. Stir in milk and vanilla. Slowly pour into custard cups. Set cups in water in shallow baking dish and bake 50-60 minutes in 350 degree oven. The custard is done when inserted knife comes out clean. Chill and invert onto serving plate by loosening with knife along edges.

Serves 4   Oakhurst Dairy

The Apple Crisp

This recipe transcends all other apple crisp recipes.

1 cup graham cracker crumbs
1 tablespoon flour
1 cup chopped pecans
1 cup brown sugar
¼ cup granulated sugar
1 tablespoon freshly grated orange rind
Dash of salt
½ teaspoon cinnamon and nutmeg
½ cup melted butter
4 large tart apples (early Macs, best)

Preheat oven to 350 degrees

Mix first five ingredients. Season with orange rind, salt, cinnamon and nutmeg. Add with melted butter. Lightly butter dish. Peel, core and thinly slice apples and place slices on bottom of dish. Scatter crumb mixture over top and bake in 350 degree oven for 45 minutes. May serve with ice cream, frozen yogurt or sweetened whipped cream.

Serves 6   Barbara Y. Sturgeon

Apple Cheese Torte

May be prepared ahead and frozen.

½   cup margarine
⅓   and ¼ and ⅓ cup sugar
¾   teaspoon vanilla
1   cup flour
1   8-ounce package cream cheese, softened
1   egg
4   cups sliced apples (4-5)
½   teaspoon cinnamon
¼   cup slivered almonds

Preheat oven to 450 degrees

Cream margarine and ⅓ cup sugar, add ¼ teaspoon vanilla. Blend in flour and spread the dough on bottom and 1½" up the sides of a 9" spring form pan. Combine softened cream cheese and ¼ cup sugar. Add 1 egg and remaining ½ teaspoon vanilla and blend well. Pour in pan, place sliced apples on top. Sprinkle with almonds. Bake in 450 degree oven for 10 minutes. Turn oven down to 400 degrees and continue baking for 25 minutes. This torte rises only 2-3" high.

Helene S. Perry

Serving sizes vary considerably,
depending on ingredients and appetites.

January Blueberry Torte

Having frozen your harvested berries, enjoy them at your fireside in January.

2	tablespoons butter
¾	cup sugar
1	egg, well-beaten
	Pinch of salt
1	egg yolk
¾	cup flour
1	teaspoon baking powder
½	"eggshell" of water
1	cup fresh blueberries

Preheat oven to 325 degrees

Cream butter with ¼ cup sugar. Add well beaten egg, salt, flour and baking powder. Add ½ "eggshell" water. Spread mixture in shallow, greased 9" baking dish. Add 1 cup blueberries, spreading evenly. Mix thoroughly 1 egg yolk with ½ cup sugar. Spread over blueberries. Bake at 325 degrees for 40 minutes approximately.

Judy Ribeiro

Fabulous Wild Blueberry Sauce

Easy and delicious. Use to top ice cream or for blueberry shortcake with whipped cream.

4	cups fresh picked blueberries, washed
½	cup sugar
2	tablespoons lemon juice
	Pinch salt
	Dash cinnamon
	Dash nutmeg
2	tablespoons flour
½	pint cream, whipped

Place berries in pot on low heat. When juice starts to ooze, sprinkle flour over berries. Stir. Add sugar, lemon juice and spices. Cook gently just until thick and berries maintain their shape. Pour over shortcakes and plop on whipped fresh cream (½ pint).

Serves 8   Manny Morgan

Blueberry Betty

I cook ahead and reheat to serve.

4   cups cubed day-old bread
¾   cup melted butter or margarine
2   cups fresh blueberries
2   tablespoons lemon juice
¼   cup sugar
1   teaspoon ground allspice
½   cup brown sugar

Preheat oven to 350 degrees

Combine bread, butter, sugar and allspice. Mix lightly. Sprinkle berries with lemon juice and brown sugar. Alternate layers of bread cubes and blueberries (start with bread cubes on bottom and end with them on top) in a greased 9" dish. Bake at 350 degrees for 20 to 30 minutes. Serve with cream or ice cream.

Serves 6   Barbara Pratt

Strawberry Sauce: whir 1 pint of strawberries, 1 teaspoon lemon juice, 2 tablespoons currant jelly and 1 cup sugar in a food processor. Freezes well.

Claremont Hotel Blueberry Crisp

1 quart blueberries
⅓ cup white sugar
½ lemon, juiced
¼ cup butter or margarine
½ teaspoon cinnamon
⅓ cup brown sugar, packed
⅓ cup flour
¾ cup quick cooking oats

Preheat oven to 375 degrees

Place blueberries in 1½ quart baking dish. Sprinkle with sugar, lemon juice and cinnamon. Cream butter and brown sugar. Blend in flour with fork. Mix in the oats. Spread over the blueberries. Bake at 375 degrees for 35-40 minutes. Serve with whipped cream or ice cream.

Serves 6 to 8   Billie McIntire, Chef
Claremont Hotel, Southwest Harbor

Honeydew Wedges with Sherbet and Blueberries

Easy and beautiful summertime dessert.

1 tablespoon cornstarch
½ cup cold water
1½ cups blueberries
¼ cup sugar
2 tablespoons crème de cassis
1 tablespoon lemon juice
¼ teaspoon cinnamon
½ medium honeydew, seeded and quartered
Lemon sherbet

Dissolve cornstarch in cold water. Combine with berries and sugar in a medium saucepan. Cook over medium heat, stirring constantly, until mixture thickens and bubbles for two minutes. Refrigerate until cold, stirring occasionally. Stir in cassis, lemon juice and cinnamon into chilled

berry mixture. To prepare honeydew wedge, cut under the fruit lengthwise to separate it from the rind. Then cut into crosswise slices about
half an inch wide. To serve, place small balls of sherbet on each
honeydew wedge and pour blueberry sauce generously over the top.

Serves 4   Nonie Pierce

All Season Fruit Torte

*I have used many different fruits and berries and glazed this with
melted quince, currant or apricot jelly.*

1	stick unsalted butter, room temperature
1	cup sugar
2	eggs
1	teaspoon vanilla
1	cup flour
	Pinch of salt
1	teaspoon baking powder
	Fruit or berries, at least 4 cups

Preheat oven to 350 degrees

Cream butter and sugar, add eggs, vanilla and blend. Add flour, baking
powder and salt (if using processor, do not over process—pulse to
blend). Spread into greased pan and cover with fruit. (Sprinkle with
cinnamon sugar, optional). Bake in oven at 350 degrees for approximately 1 hour.

Serves 6 to 8   Janet Smaldon

*If espresso powder is unavailable,
use twice the amount of instant coffee.*

Baked Pears Ulla (Oolah)

A simple, delicious old favorite.

1 tablespoon soft butter
⅓ cup apricot jam
2 to 3 macaroons
3 to 4 firm, ripe pears
¼ cup dry vermouth

Preheat oven to 350 degrees

Peel, quarter and core the pears, then slice them into ⅜" thick pieces. Arrange in shallow baking dish. Force jam through sieve, combine with vermouth and pour over pears. Crumble macaroons over pears. Dot with butter. Bake for 20-25 minutes at 350 degrees, until lightly brown. Serve hot or cold with light cream.

Oranges Grande Bretagne

Wonderful light dessert!

4 navel oranges
1 cup sugar
2 tablespoons currant jelly
½ cup water (sugar, jelly and water to be boiled together for 15 minutes)

Using a zester, remove rind of 2 oranges, making sure there is no white on orange zest. In fresh water each time, boil zest 3 times, 10 minutes per time. Put aside. With sharp knife, pare oranges, removing all membrane. Slice peeled oranges and pour boiling syrup over the fruit. Let rest 15 minutes. Strain and boil syrup with jelly again for 10 minutes. Pour over fruit again. Add zest. Chill and serve.

Serves 4   Tinker Barron

Orange Peach Sherbet

Quick and easy. Best if eaten within a few days. Does not keep flavor for a long time in the freezer.

1   cup buttermilk
¼   cup concentrated frozen orange juice
3   cups sliced fresh peaches
1   cup sugar

Place all ingredients in food processor. Blend until smooth. Pour into freezer tray and return to freezer. When frozen ½" from sides, stir until smooth, refreeze.

Makes about 1 quart.

Susan Donnell Konkel
Trustee

Russian Raspberry Pudding

This is a traditional Russian recipe.

2   cups fresh raspberries
2   eggs
1   cup sour cream
1   tablespoon sugar
1   tablespoon flour

Preheat oven to 350 degrees

Place raspberries in baking dish and put in preheated oven while beating the following: sour cream with eggs, sugar and flour. Pour mixture over berries. Bake at 350 degrees for 40-45 minutes until firm and lightly browned. Serve warm or at room temperature.

Cecile Carver

Pineapple Soufflé

This is a mouth-watering dessert which is always a winner at dinner parties.

6 slices white bread cut into 1" cubes (freeze bread before cutting)
1½ sticks butter or margarine
2 eggs
¾ cup sugar
¼ cup flour
1 16-ounce can crushed pineapple

Preheat oven to 350 degrees

Brown bread cubes in butter or margarine in medium frying pan. Mix eggs, sugar and flour together and stir thoroughly in separate dish. Grease bottom of Pyrex dish or regular baking pan and put in pineapple with egg, sugar and flour mixture poured together. Put cubes of browned bread on top of pineapple topping mixture and bake at 350 degrees for 35 to 40 minutes.

Serves 6 to 8

David C. Driskell
Artist

Pecan Strawberry Shortcake

Shortcake:
2 cups all purpose flour
½ cup finely ground pecans
¼ cup sugar
2 teaspoons baking powder
½ cup butter
1 egg, beaten
⅔ cup milk
1 tablespoon finely grated orange peel
Strawberries:
6 cups sliced strawberries
¼ cup sugar

Fresh Sliced Oranges with Raspberry Sauce

A light dessert. Nice balance to a dinner.

4   large navel oranges, chilled
1   pint fresh raspberries (or
    strawberries, stemmed), chilled
2   tablespoons sugar
1   tablespoon Kirsch

Peel oranges, including white pulp, and slice into 5 or 6 even slices. Put berries, sugar and Kirsch into blender and purée 10 seconds. Serve oranges and spoon sauce over it.

Serves 4   Marguerite Rafter

Cranberry Pudding

This is a family favorite. A wonderful combination of sweet and tart.

1½ tablespoons butter
1   cup sugar
½   cup milk
1   cup flour
1½ teaspoons baking powder
2   cups raw cranberries

Preheat oven to 375 degrees

Cream the butter and sugar. Add the milk, flour and baking powder. Add the cranberries. Pour into buttered and floured dish. Bake at 375 degrees for 30 minutes. Serve with vanilla sauce.

Vanilla Sauce:
1   stick butter
1   cup sugar
    A little vanilla
½   cup cream

Combine all ingredients in the top of a double boiler until sugar is melted. Add cream and stir. Serve warm over cranberry pudding.

Serves 6   Lisa Witte

Cranberry Pecan Pie

1   cup sugar
1½ tablespoons flour
¼   cup softened butter
2   eggs
¾   cup light corn syrup
¼   teaspoon salt
1   teaspoon vanilla
1   teaspoon orange peel, grated
½   teaspoon nutmeg
1   cup pecans (or walnuts), chopped
1   cup fresh or frozen cranberries
1   9-inch pastry shell
     Whipped cream, optional

Preheat oven to 350 degrees

Cream together sugar, flour and butter. Add eggs, corn syrup, salt, vanilla, orange peel and nutmeg. Beat until well blended. Stir in nuts and cranberries. Pour into unbaked 9-inch pastry shell. Bake in preheated 350 degree oven 60 to 70 minutes or until knife inserted in center comes out clean. If desired, serve with a dollop of whipped cream.

Serves 7 to 8   Mary Haggerty
Lincoln House Country Inn, Dennysville

*Skier's Delight: fill a mason jar with pitted prunes,
cover with rum, and let soak until wrinkles are
gone. Drain and pack prunes in a container for a
zippy outdoor winter pick-me-up.*

Angela's Apple-Cranberry Pie

This recipe was awarded a Grand Prize in the 1990 Yankee Magazine Competition.

Crust:
  2½ cups flour
  ½   teaspoon salt
  1   cup vegetable shortening
      Ice water, approximately 8 to 10
      tablespoons
Cranberry Base:
  2   cups cranberries
  1   cup sugar
  ½   cup orange juice
  ½   cup water
      Zest from one orange
      Dash nutmeg
Apple Filling:
  8   to 10 Cortland apples
  ⅓   cup flour
  1   teaspoon cinnamon
  ¾   teaspoon nutmeg
      Pinch salt
  1   cup sugar
  5   to 6 pats butter

Preheat oven to 400 degrees

Crust: prepare crust in classic tradition. Cut shortening into flour and salt. Add tablespoons of ice water to mixture and stir with fingers until the mixture is moist and able to stick together. Chill for about an hour in a damp cloth.

Cranberry Base: cook cranberry mixture over low heat until the cranberries begin to pop. Cool and drain most of the juice.

Apple Filling: peel apples and cut into thin slices. Mix dry ingredients and pour over apples. Gently toss until the apple slices are covered.

Divide pastry dough in half. Roll out the bottom half and place in 10" glass pie plate. Pour the cranberry mixture over the crust and then place the apples over the cranberries. Place the pats of butter over the apples. Roll out the remaining dough and moisten the edge of the bottom crust with water so that when you place the top crust on the bottom, the edges will seal much better. Press edges firmly and trim excess crust. Make your favorite roll edge. Moisten the top of the pie with a little milk and sprinkle with sugar. Cut slits on pie top and bake. Bake for at least 50 minutes in 400 degree oven. When baking two pies, be certain to rotate the pies so that they will brown evenly.

Angela LeBlanc

Ice Cream Pecan Pumpkin Pie à la Leona

An unusual and interesting variation on the pumpkin pie.

¼	cup honey or brown sugar
¾	cup canned or mashed, cooked pumpkin
½	teaspoon cinnamon
¼	teaspoon ginger
	Dash nutmeg
	Dash cloves
¼	teaspoon salt
3	cups vanilla ice cream (or frozen yogurt)
⅓	cup chopped pecans
1	9" baked graham cracker pie shell

Combine honey, pumpkin, spices, and salt. Bring just to a boil, stirring constantly. Cool. Beat ingredients into softened ice cream. Add nuts. Spread in pie shell and freeze until firm. Optional: serve with sweetened whipped cream. Garnish with chocolate curls.

Serves 6 to 8   Barbara Y. Sturgeon

Blend equal parts of marshmallow fluff, sour cream and the liqueur of your choice and serve with summer fruit.

Maine Blueberry Pudding Cake

Robert P. Tristram Coffin, Harpswell-born Pulitzer Prize poet, said of blueberries, "They have the powder of the sky on their fresh sides." He added, "A blueberry needs heat to bring out its best points." If you live or visit in Maine you know we are partial to steamed blueberry puddings.

2   cups fresh blueberries
1   cup flour
1   teaspoon baking powder
¼   teaspoon salt
3   tablespoons melted shortening
1¾ cups sugar
½   cup milk
1   tablespoon cornstarch
1   cup boiling water

Preheat oven to 350 degrees

Place blueberries in bottom of 8" x 8" pan. In a bowl, combine flour, baking powder, salt, shortening, ¾ cup sugar and milk. Pour batter over the berries. Mix the remaining cup of sugar and cornstarch. Sprinkle evenly over the batter. Pour the boiling water over all. DO NOT MIX. Bake for 45 minutes in 350 degree oven. Serve hot or at room temperature with whipped cream or ice cream, if desired.

Serves 6 to 8   Beatrice H. Comas

Upside Down Date Pudding

1   cup chopped dates
1   cup boiling water
½   cup granulated sugar
½   cup brown sugar
1   egg
2   tablespoons butter, melted
1½ cups sifted flour
½   teaspoon salt
1   teaspoon baking soda
½   teaspoon baking powder
½   cup walnuts

1½ cups brown sugar
1   tablespoon butter
1½ cups boiling water

Preheat oven to 375 degrees

Combine dates and 1 cup boiling water. Cool. In mixing bowl, blend granulated sugar, ½ cup brown sugar, egg and 2 tablespoons butter. Sift next four ingredients. Add to sugar mixture. Add nuts and cooled dates. Pour into baking pan. Combine 1½ cups brown sugar, butter and boiling water. Pour over date mixture. Bake at 375 degrees for 40 minutes. Cut and invert onto serving plate. Serve warm. Pass cream to pour over pudding, if desired.

Serves 9 to 12   Mary Haggerty
Lincoln House Country Inn, Dennysville

Indian Pudding

Great with whipped cream or ice cream. Serve warm.

1   quart milk
½   cup yellow cornmeal
2   tablespoons melted butter
½   cup molasses
1   teaspoon salt
1   teaspoon cinnamon
¼   teaspoon ginger
2   eggs

Preheat oven to 350 degrees

Scald the milk and slowly pour in the cornmeal, stirring continuously. Cook in a double boiler for about 20 minutes. Combine butter, molasses, salt, cinnamon and ginger. Beat the eggs (add about 2 tablespoons of hot mixture to beaten eggs before adding to hot mixture in entirety). Add warmed eggs to cornmeal mixture. Add molasses mixture. Pour into greased 2 quart baking dish. Place entire dish into pan of hot water. Bake at 350 degrees for 1 hour.

Serves 8   Kristine Hoyt

Grape Nut Pudding

4 tablespoons butter
1 cup sugar
2 egg yolks
3 tablespoons lemon juice
1 tablespoon grated lemon rind
4 tablespoons flour
4 tablespoons Grape Nuts
1 cup milk
2 egg whites

Preheat oven to 325 degrees

Cream butter and sugar. Add well beaten egg yolks, lemon juice and rind. Mix well. Add flour, Grape Nuts, milk and mix well. Fold in stiff, beaten egg whites. Pour into greased quart casserole and place in a pan of hot water. Bake at 325 degrees for 1 hour, 15 minutes. Serve hot or cold.

Nancy Jahn Hartley

Sticky Scottish Toffee Pudding

This dessert was served to a Maine Audubon group at the tea shop at Haddo House outside Aberdeen in Scotland. It was so good we asked for the recipe as a souvenir of a great trip.

Pudding:
6 ounces dates
1 teaspoon baking soda
2 ounces margarine
6 ounces sugar
1 egg
8 ounces self rising flour (or regular flour plus 1 teaspoon baking soda)
Sauce:
4 ounces butter
8 ounces soft brown sugar
½ pint heavy cream

Preheat oven to 350 degrees

Pudding: chop dates and soak in ½ pint boiling water with 1 teaspoon of baking soda. Beat margarine with sugar. Add egg, flour, date water and dates. Put into 2" x 7" x 10" baking pan and bake in 350 degree oven for 40 minutes.
Sauce: melt butter and sugar slowly, then add cream and simmer for 5 minutes.

Serves 4 to 6   Thomas A. Urquhart, Executive Director
                                                  Maine Audubon Society

White Chocolate Macadamia Nut Cheesecake

Delicious!!

⅓   cup butter, melted
1¼ cups graham cracker crumbs
¼   cup sugar
2   8-ounce packages cream cheese
1   14-ounce can sweetened
     condensed milk
3   eggs
¼   cup lemon juice
16 ounces white chocolate, melted
1   cup macadamia nuts, coarsely
     chopped

Preheat oven to 300 degrees

Combine butter, graham cracker crumbs and sugar. Pat firmly on bottom of 9 inch spring form pan. Beat cream cheese until fluffy. Add sweetened condensed milk, until smooth. Add eggs and lemon juice. Add 10 ounces of melted white chocolate and ¾ cup chopped macadamia nuts. Pour into prepared pan. Bake 50-55 minutes at 300 degrees or until cake springs back when lightly touched. Cool to room temperature. Remove sides of pan. Spread remaining melted white chocolate on top. Garnish with remaining crushed macadamia nuts.

                                                              Mary M. Yeo

Raspberry Cheesecake

An elegant dessert which can be prepared in about 15 minutes. It may also be prepared a day in advance.

Crust:
- 1¾ cups graham cracker crumbs
- ½ cup sugar
- ¼ cup chopped nuts
- 1 teaspoon cinnamon
- ½ cup butter

Filling:
- 3 eggs
- 2 8-ounce packages cream cheese
- 1 cup sugar
- 2 teaspoons vanilla
- Dash salt
- 3 cups sour cream

Topping:
- 1 10-ounce package raspberries
- 1 tablespoon cornstarch

Preheat oven to 325 degrees

Combine graham cracker crumbs, ½ cup sugar, ¼ cup nuts, 1 teaspoon cinnamon and ½ cup butter. Press into 8" spring form pan, on the bottom, and up the sides. Mix eggs, softened cream cheese, 1 cup sugar, vanilla, salt and sour cream until smooth. Pour into crust lined pan. Bake at 325 degrees for 45 minutes or until firm (it will still jiggle). Heat raspberries and corn starch until thick. Spread on top of cheesecake when both topping and cake have cooled. Chill for several hours before serving.

Serves 12

Kit Farnsworth

Cakes, Bars and Cookies

Rotunda of
L. D. M. Sweat Memorial Galleries

Apple Cake

2 eggs
1 cup white sugar
1 cup brown sugar
1¼ cups vegetable oil
2 teaspoons vanilla
3 cups flour
1 teaspoon soda
1 teaspoon cinnamon
½ teaspoon salt
3 cups chopped apple
1 cup chopped walnuts
Granulated or confectioners'
sugar for dust

Preheat oven to 375 degrees

In a large bowl, combine eggs with sugar, vanilla and oil. Stir in flour, soda, cinnamon and salt. Add apples and walnuts. The mixture will be stiff. Turn into greased Bundt pan or large tube pan. Bake at 375 degrees for one hour. Test with a piece of uncooked spaghetti! It should be dry in the middle and pulling away from the pan a little. Let cool before inverting onto plate. Dust with granulated or confectioners' sugar.

Serves 12 to 18

June Pattenaude's Carrot Pineapple Cake

1½ cups flour
1 cup granulated sugar
¼ cup brown sugar, packed
1 teaspoon baking powder
1 teaspoon baking soda
1 teaspoon ground cinnamon
Dash allspice
½ teaspoon salt
⅔ cup oil
2 eggs
1 teaspoon vanilla
1 cup shredded carrots

½ cup crushed pineapple with syrup
1 cup raisins
¼ cup finely chopped walnuts
Powdered sugar

Preheat oven to 350 degrees

Stir together flour, granulated sugar, brown sugar, baking powder, baking soda, cinnamon, allspice and salt. Add oil, eggs, vanilla, carrots and pineapple with syrup. Blend until moist, then beat one minute. Stir in raisins and walnuts. Pour into greased and floured 9" square baking pan. Bake at 350 degrees for 35 minutes. Cool 10 minutes, then remove from pan. Pierce top of cake at 1 inch intervals with fork. Combine powdered sugar with enough water to make a very thin glaze. Drizzle over warm cake and allow to stand until glaze penetrates cake and gives sheen to top.

Serves 10

Richard Pattenaude
President, University of Southern Maine

McLellan Cake

From Miss Charlotte McLellan - 1972. This was served at the McLellan-Sweat House for teas.

1 package Betty Crocker yellow cake mix
1 package instant vanilla pudding
4 whole eggs, beaten
¾ cup dry sherry
¾ cup Crisco
1 tablespoon or more fresh grated nutmeg

Preheat oven to 350 degrees

Mix well. Beat 5 minutes. Bake in greased angel food pan for 45 minutes at 350 degrees. Cool in pan before taking out. Bon appetit!

Portland Museum of Art

Judy's Cake

This cake is a snap to assemble.

Cake:
2¼ cups flour
2 cups sugar
½ teaspoon baking soda
1 teaspoon vanilla
½ pound butter, softened
3 large eggs
8 ounces plain yogurt

Filling:
Select and combine ½ cup each of 2 or 3 of the following: raisins, mini chocolate chips, chopped pecans, coconut, brickle, or butterscotch bits

Preheat oven to 325 degrees

Cream butter and sugar, add eggs, then yogurt. Combine flour, baking soda and add to butter mixture, then vanilla. Butter and flour Bundt tube pan. Pour half the batter into the pan, add your fillings, then the other half. Bake in 325 degree oven for 1 hour, maybe 10 minutes more, until done. Cool for 10 minutes and then turn out of pan.

Sandra Scully

Gateau Royale with Crème Chantilly

Very rich; serve with strawberries marinated in Grand Marnier.

Cake:
8 ounces unsweetened chocolate
8 ounces sweet butter
4 eggs
1 cup sugar
6 tablespoons cornstarch
2 tablespoons Grand Marnier

Sauce:

1   cup heavy cream
½   cup powdered sugar
2   tablespoons Cointreau

Preheat oven to 325 degrees

Melt chocolate in double boiler and cool. Cream butter in processor until light and fluffy. Beat eggs until fluffy and add sugar. Then add cooled chocolate and butter to processor, also cornstarch and liquor. Blend. Pour into buttered ring mold, place in large pan and add water ½ way up mold. Bake at 325 degrees for 45 minutes to 1 hour until knife inserted comes clean. Cool. Lift onto platter only when cool. Put bowl in freezer ½ hour before whipping cream and sugar, stir in Cointreau and serve with Gateau.

Serves 8 or more   Cecile Carver

German Plain Cake

So simple and delicious. Dictates a tea party!

2   tablespoons butter
1   egg, beaten
2   cups sugar
1   cup milk
3½ cups flour
1   heaping tablespoon baking powder
     Grated rind of 1 large lemon
     Confectioners' sugar

Preheat oven to 350 degrees

Cream butter and sugar, add beaten egg and mix. Add flour and baking powder alternately with milk. Fold in lemon rind. Place in a loaf cake pan and bake in 350 degree oven for 50 minutes. Cool 10 minutes before turning out. Sift confectioners' sugar over exterior once it has cooled.

D. Lombard Brett

Old Fashioned Gingerbread

This is a 100-year-old recipe from my mother.

½ cup butter or other shortening
½ cup sugar
1 egg, beaten
2½ cups flour, sifted
1½ teaspoons baking soda
1 teaspoon cinnamon
1 teaspoon ginger
½ teaspoon cloves
½ teaspoon salt
1 cup molasses
1 cup hot water

Preheat oven to 350 degrees

Cream shortening and sugar. Add beaten egg. Measure and sift dry ingredients. Mix molasses with hot water. Add dry ingredients alternately with liquid, beating after each addition. Pour into greased and floured 9" x 9" x 2" pan, and bake 45 minutes in 350 degree oven.

Zella B. Thomas

Gingerbread à la Wadsworth-Longfellow House

Henry Wadsworth Longfellow, while a student at Bowdoin College, wrote his parents on September 22, 1822, "I am much pleased with college life… " and requested cotton stockings, apples, pears and tooth powder. A special request, "Tell the girls to send a whole parcel of gingerbread with them."

½ cup butter or margarine
½ cup brown sugar
1 egg
1 cup molasses
¼ cup freshly grated ginger root
2½ cups flour
1 teaspoon cinnamon

1½ teaspoons baking soda
1   cup boiling water

Preheat oven to 350 degrees

Cream the butter with the sugar. Beat the egg and add to the butter. Beat in the molasses and ginger root. In a separate bowl, stir together the flour, cinnamon and baking soda. Beat the flour mixture into the ginger mixture. Add the boiling water and blend. Turn the batter into a greased and floured 8" x 8" pan or tube pan. Bake the cake at 350 degrees for 50 minutes or until it tests done with a toothpick. Let cool on a rack.

Serves 8 to 10

Elizabeth Miller
Director, Maine Historical Society

Quick Chocolate Cake

A great time saver. Goes together in minutes. Makes a very moist cake.

1½ cups flour
1   cup sugar
3   tablespoons cocoa
1   teaspoon baking soda
½   teaspoon salt
⅓   cup cooking oil
1   tablespoon vinegar
1   teaspoon vanilla
1   cup cold water

Preheat oven to 350 degrees

Sift flour, sugar, cocoa, baking soda and salt into a 9" greased pan. Make 3 holes in mixture. Pour oil into one hole, vinegar in another, and vanilla in third. Pour cup of water over all and mix with a fork until dry ingredients disappear. Bake in 350 degree oven for 30 minutes. Cool. Use your favorite frosting. Frost in pan; do not turn out! I often just sprinkle chopped nuts on top.

Serves 9 to 12

Neva L. Beck

plates. Spoon some strawberries with their juice onto each one, then some whipped cream. Gently place each top on the cream and sift confectioners' sugar lightly over the whole plate.

Cafe Always, Portland

Katahdin Cake

Very moist. Easy to make. The frosting is a delicious must.

Cake:
1   stick margarine
4   tablespoons cocoa
1   cup water
½   cup vegetable oil
2   cups flour
1   teaspoon vanilla
2   cups sugar
½   cup buttermilk
2   tablespoons baking soda
2   eggs

Frosting:
1   stick margarine
⅓   cup buttermilk
Dash of salt
4   tablespoons cocoa
2   cups confectioners' sugar

Preheat oven to 400 degrees

Cake: in saucepan, mix cocoa, water, margarine and bring to a boil. Remove from stove. Add, all at once, rest of ingredients, eggs last. Beat slowly until smooth. Pour into ungreased 13" x 9" pan and bake 25 to 30 minutes in 400 degree oven. Remove from oven and frost while still hot. Cut when cool.
Frosting: bring all ingredients except sugar to a boil and stir. Remove from heat and add sugar. Frosting can be as thick or thin as desired.

Serves 12   Vera Lagomarsino

Old Fashioned Chocolate Cake

A never fail recipe. Can be halved.

Cake:
1   cup boiling water
4   squares Baker's chocolate
½   cup butter
2   cups flour
2   cups sugar
1½ teaspoons baking soda
2   eggs
½   cup sour milk (add 2 drops
     vinegar to sour)
1½ teaspoons vanilla

Frosting:
2   squares Baker's chocolate
5   tablespoons hot water
1   tablespoon butter
1   teaspoon vanilla
½   to ¾ box confectioners' sugar

Preheat oven to 350 degrees

Cake: melt the chocolate and the butter over boiling water. Sift together into a big bowl the flour, sugar and baking soda. Beat into the flour mixture the eggs, sour milk and vanilla. Stir in the melted chocolate mixture. Divide between two greased round tins and bake in 350 degree oven for approximately 30 minutes. When done, cool and invert on wire rack.

Frosting: melt the chocolate, hot water and butter. Whisk in the vanilla and enough confectioners' sugar to reach spreading consistency. Beat with whisk until shiny and spread as a filling and a top frosting. May be flavored with a pinch of instant coffee, if desired.

Ellen Higgins

Yogurt Spice Cake

Cake:

½ cup butter
1½ cups sugar
3 eggs, beaten
2 cups flour
1 teaspoon baking powder
1 teaspoon baking soda
¼ teaspoon salt
1 teaspoon nutmeg
½ teaspoon cinnamon
1 cup plain yogurt
½ teaspoon vanilla

Topping:

1 tablespoon butter
½ cup brown sugar
½ cup finely chopped walnuts
¼ teaspoon vanilla
¾ cup shredded coconut
¼ cup cream

Preheat oven to 325 degrees

Cake: in a large mixing bowl cream the butter and sugar until smooth. Beat in the eggs. Sift together the dry ingredients. Add alternately with the yogurt to the butter mixture. Add the vanilla and blend well. Pour into a greased and floured 9" x 13" baking pan. Bake 45 minutes in 325 degree oven or until a cake tester comes out clean. Remove from the oven and cool.

Topping: mix together the butter and brown sugar. Add the remaining ingredients and blend well. Spread the mixture evenly over the cooled cake. Place briefly under the broiler until lightly browned, watching closely to prevent burning.

Serves 6

*Fresh ginger, placed in a jar covered
with sherry, will keep for months in the refrigerator.*

Raspberry Bar Cookie

Great for everyone, especially kids! These can be made with strawberry jam as well.

¾ cup seedless raspberry jam
½ cup butter, room temperature
½ cup light brown sugar
1 cup flour
⅛ teaspoon salt
¼ teaspoon baking soda
1 cup rolled oats

Preheat oven to 350 degrees

Grease 8" square pan. Mix all dry ingredients. Take 2 cups of mixture and press into bottom of pan. Spread jam and then sprinkle remaining mixture over top. Press lightly. Bake in 350 degree oven for 35 to 40 minutes. Allow to cool before cutting.

Yield: 24 2½" bars   Phyllis Klein

Ranch Cookies

½ cup melted shortening
½ cup brown sugar
½ cup white sugar
1 egg, unbeaten
½ cup coconut (coarse)
½ cup oatmeal
1 cup flour
1 cup cornflakes
1 teaspoon baking powder
½ teaspoon salt
1 teaspoon vanilla

Preheat oven to 350 degrees

Mix thoroughly. Form into small balls. Mash with fork and place on ungreased cookie sheet. Bake in 350 degree oven for 10 to 12 minutes.

Nut Roll with Caramel Sauce

This is from the Kennedy Center's cookbook and was submitted by Conductor Max Rudolf who has summered in Maine on Mt. Desert Island. The sauce is my addition.

Nut roll:

½	cup sugar
4	eggs, separated
4	ounces ground walnuts
½	pint heavy cream
4	tablespoons powered sugar

Caramel sauce:

½	cup brown sugar
½	cup light corn syrup
2	tablespoons butter
1	teaspoon vanilla
½	cup light cream

Preheat oven to 350 degrees

Nut roll: beat egg yolk with granulated sugar. Fold in stiffly beaten egg whites and ground walnuts. Spread mixture on buttered and floured parchment (or wax) paper on large cookie sheet. Bake at 350 degrees for 15 to 18 minutes. Turn the cake over onto a dish towel sprinkled with powdered sugar and then peel off the wax paper while still hot. When cooled, spread with whipped cream. Roll and top with powdered sugar. Refrigerate several hours before serving. Slice and serve with caramel sauce, prepared as follows.

Caramel sauce: cook brown sugar and corn syrup in double boiler for 10 minutes to blend, then add light cream. Cook 30 minutes in double boiler, stirring occasionally. Add butter and vanilla. Serve warm or cold. If too thick, add a little more cream.

Serves 8   Mae R. Rossow

When substituting vegetable oil for vegetable shortening, butter or margarine, use one-third less.

Real Brownies

Brownie lovers are always trying new recipes, but I am stuck on this one. No other brownie has the intensity of these!

4   squares unsweetened baking chocolate
2   sticks unsalted butter
4   eggs, beaten
2   cups sugar
1   cup flour
½   teaspoon salt
½   teaspoon vanilla
¼   teaspoon almond extract (optional)

Preheat oven to 275 degrees

Butter and then put wax paper in a 9" x 13" pan. Place chocolate and butter in large saucepan and melt over low heat. Add to chocolate and stir well: eggs, sugar, flour, salt and vanilla and almond extract (optional). Turn into prepared pan and bake in 275 degree oven for 1 hour. When cool, cut into squares. Store in refrigerator, if there are any left.

Yield: 24 large brownies   Sarah Marshall

Toffee Bars

These are good and easy.

1   cup margarine
½   cup brown sugar
½   cup white sugar
1   large egg yolk
1½   cups flour
12   ounces chocolate chips
      Sliced almonds to sprinkle on chocolate, about ¾ cup

Preheat oven to 325 degrees

Cream margarine and sugars until fluffy. Add egg yolk and mix well, gradually adding flour and mix until incorporated. Pat into 8" square pan. You may need extra flour because it is soft and sticky. Bake 25 minutes or until barely golden around edges. After removing from oven, sprinkle chocolate chips on top and let them melt for several minutes, spread with spatula. Sprinkle sliced almonds over the chocolate. Let sit to cool. You may need to chill in freezer for 5 minutes to set enough to cut into bars.

Peggy Osher
Trustee

Neiman's $250.00 Cookies

The cookies are delightful.

2	cups butter
2	cups brown sugar
2	teaspoons vanilla
5	cups oatmeal
1	teaspoon salt
2	teaspoons baking soda
1	8-ounce grated Hershey Bar (candy)
4	cups flour
2	cups sugar
4	eggs
2	teaspoons baking powder
24	ounces semi-sweet chocolate chips
3	cups chopped nuts

Preheat oven to 375 degrees

Measure oatmeal and blend in blender to a fine powder. Cream butter and both sugars. Add eggs and vanilla. Mix together with flour, oatmeal, salt, baking powder and soda. Add chips, candy and nuts. Refrigerate for ½ hour. Roll into balls and place 2" apart on cookie sheet. Bake in 375 degree oven for approximately 6 minutes. This recipe may be halved.

Yield: 170   Prudence D. Gilmore

Pecan Pie Bars

¼ cup butter, room temperature
⅓ cup plus ¼ cup packed brown sugar
1 cup plus 2 tablespoons flour
¼ teaspoon baking powder
1 cup chopped pecans
2 eggs, beaten
¾ cup heavy corn syrup
½ teaspoon salt
1 teaspoon vanilla

Preheat oven to 350 degrees

Cream butter and ⅓ cup brown sugar. Beat in 1 cup flour and baking powder until mixture becomes crumbly. Add ¼ cup pecans. Pat into 12" x 8" pan. Bake 10 minutes. Beat eggs until foamy. Add corn syrup, remaining ¼ cup brown sugar, 2 tablespoons flour, salt and vanilla. Mix well. Pour over the baked crust. Sprinkle with remaining ¾ cup pecans. Bake in 350 degree oven for 25-30 minutes. Cool. Cut into bars.

Yield: 24 bars

Ann Willauer
President of the Museum Guild

Snickerdoodles

1 cup shortening or margarine
1½ cups sugar
2 eggs
2¾ cups flour
2 teaspoons cream of tartar
1 teaspoon soda
½ teaspoon salt
2 tablespoons sugar
1 teaspoon cinnamon
Pecan halves (optional)

Preheat oven to 400 degrees

Cream sugar and margarine. Add one egg at a time and beat well. Stir in flour, cream of tartar and salt. Roll dough into balls the size of a walnut.

Mix sugar and cinnamon, rolling each ball in mixture. Press a pecan half on each dough ball, if desired. Put on a cookie sheet 2" apart and bake until lightly browned but still soft, 8-10 minutes in 400 degree oven.

Makes 4 dozen 2½" cookies   Marian J. Baker

Paradise Cookies

These cookies are chewy and moist in spite of the stiff dough.

1	stick butter, softened
1	stick corn oil margarine, softened
¾	cup brown sugar
¾	cup sugar
2	eggs, beaten
1	teaspoon vanilla
⅓	cup coconut
2	cups flour
1	teaspoon baking soda
1	teaspoon salt
3½	ounces macadamia nuts, chopped
12	ounce bag milk chocolate chips

Preheat oven to 400 degrees

Cream butter, margarine and sugar together. Add eggs and vanilla. Mix well. Stir in coconut. Add flour, baking soda and salt. Mix well. Batter will be stiff. Add nuts and chocolate chips. Drop generously sized tablespoons of dough onto cookie sheet (16 to a sheet). Bake in 400 degree oven for 8 to 10 minutes. Cool on sheets, then transfer to rack.

Yield: 48 cookies   LuAnn Perakis

*Grind nuts quickly by crushing
them with a rolling pin or wooden mallet.*

Cheesecake Bars

2 cups Oreo cookies, finely crushed (about 25 cookies)
3 8-ounce packages of cream cheese, softened
3 tablespoons margarine, melted
1 14-ounce can sweetened condensed milk
3 eggs, beaten
2 teaspoons vanilla extract
2 1-ounce squares unsweetened chocolate

Preheat oven to 300 degrees.

Mix crushed cookies and melted margarine. Press cookie mixture into bottom of a 13" x 9" baking pan. Press firmly. Beat cream cheese until fluffy. Beat in sweetened condensed milk. Beat until smooth. Add vanilla and eggs. Mix well. Pour half the batter evenly over cookie crust. Stir melted chocolate into remaining batter and pour over batter in pan. To marble, swirl knife through batter. Cook in 300 degree oven for 45 to 50 minutes. Cool and cut into bars.

Greg Welch
Artist

Oatmeal Lace Cookies

The ingredients are very simple but strict. The cookies burn very easily.

½ pound butter, melted (don't let it bubble)
2¼ cups Quick Quaker Oats
2¼ cups brown sugar
3 tablespoons flour
½ teaspoon salt
1 egg, slightly beaten
1 teaspoon vanilla

Preheat oven to 350 degrees

Mix melted butter into dry ingredients. Let sugar melt. Add egg and vanilla. Let mixture stand overnight or for several hours so oats can thoroughly absorb sugar and butter. As a result, the mix will bubble in the hot oven and the lacy holes will appear. The procedure is simple, once you have tried it, and the mix will keep for weeks in the refrigerator. Scoop by spoonfuls onto cookie sheets and flatten to size of a thick 50¢ piece. Bake in 350 degree oven for 10+ minutes. Cookies are done when they are medium amber color. They will turn a nice brown in 30 seconds in their hot pans. If they stick on the pans, put them back in the oven for half a minute. Dry cookies on a rack or on a platter.

Yield: 36 to 48 cookies, depending on size   Marion Lowndes

Butterscotch Cookies

The trick is to remove cookies from cookie sheet before they harden.

1½ cups flour
1   teaspoon salt
1   teaspoon baking soda
1   cup butter or margarine
¾   cup brown sugar
¾   cup white sugar
2   eggs, beaten
1   teaspoon vanilla extract
1   large package butterscotch bits
    (chocolate or peanut butter bits
    may be substituted)

Preheat oven to 375 degrees

Sift first three ingredients. Melt butter or margarine in double boiler and add sugars. Beat eggs slightly. Stir together until smooth: flour, butter, sugar mixture and eggs. Add 1 teaspoon vanilla extract. Fold in butterscotch chips. Drop 1 teaspoon at a time on cookie sheet (12 to a sheet). Bake in 375 degree oven for 10 to 12 minutes.

Yield: 48 to 60 cookies   Beth Wiggins

Almond Tuiles

Really delicious and not at all difficult.

½   cup sugar
2½ tablespoons all purpose flour
2   large egg whites, whisked with
    a fork
⅔   cup blanched sliced almonds
½   to 1 teaspoon almond extract

Preheat oven to 400 degrees.

In bowl combine well the sugar, egg white and flour. Stir in almonds and extract gently. Chill batter at least 2 hours or overnight. Spoon rounded teaspoons of batter 3" apart onto buttered and floured baking sheets. Flatten with wet fork back. Bake in 400 degree oven for 8-10 minutes. Curl around rolling pin to make cylinders. If they're too stiff, put back in oven for a few seconds.

Yield: about 30   Anne Hilliard

Sugar Cookies

The thinner, the better.

¼   pound butter
1¼ cups sugar
2   eggs, beaten
1   teaspoon vanilla
2   cups flour
1½ teaspoons salt
2   teaspoons baking powder

Preheat oven to 350 degrees

Combine all ingredients. Roll out on floured cloth until you can see through (very, very thin). Use round or any shape cookie cutter. Place on ungreased cookie sheet. Sprinkle with sugar. Bake in 350 degree oven for 5 to 6 minutes.

Yield: 4 dozen cookies   Barbara Laughlin

Date Filled Cookies

Time consuming but well worth it.

Filling:

    Large package dates, cut up

  ¾ cup sugar

  ¾ cup water

  2 tablespoons lemon juice

Cookie:

  1 cup sugar

  2 tablespoons molasses

  2 eggs, beaten

  1 cup shortening

  2 tablespoons milk

  4 cups flour

  2 teaspoons cream of tartar

  1 teaspoon soda

  2 teaspoons vanilla

Preheat oven to 350 degrees

Filling: combine ingredients thoroughly and cook until thick. Let cool. Cookie: cream sugar, molasses, eggs, shortening and milk. Add other dry ingredients. Chill dough for about 1 hour. Divide dough in half. Roll out dough to ⅛" thickness and cut with cookie cutter. Place cookies on cookie sheets. Divide filling for about 1 teaspoon for each cookie. Roll out remaining dough and cover each cookie. Gently press down edges. Bake in 350 degree oven about 10 to 15 minutes until brown. Cool on wire rack.

Yield: 3 dozen cookies   Marilyn Spencer

If you have no pastry bag, cut a hole in a
corner of a Ziploc storage bag and use for piping.

Swedish Ginger Snaps

These take time but are worth it.

¾ cup margarine
1 cup sugar
1 medium egg
¼ cup molasses
1½ teaspoons cinnamon
1 teaspoon ginger
½ teaspoon cloves
2 teaspoons baking soda
2 cups flour
½ cup slivered almonds

Preheat oven to 375 degrees

Cream margarine and sugar. Add egg, molasses, spices, soda and flour. Mix well. Roll rounded ½ teaspoon of dough into balls. Flatten with bottom of glass which has been greased and dipped in sugar (dip in sugar for each cookie). Press almond sliver into cookie. Bake in 375 degree oven for 12 minutes. Remove from pan to cool.

Peggy Osher
Trustee

Maple Memory Cookies

These are a favorite of our family and friends.

2¼ cups flour
1 teaspoon baking powder
½ teaspoon soda
½ teaspoon salt
¾ cup shortening (margarine)
½ cup brown sugar
1 egg
½ cup maple syrup
1 teaspoon maple flavoring

½ cup chopped walnuts plus
walnut halves for decoration

Preheat oven to 400 degrees

Sift together flour, baking powder, soda and salt. Cream shortening and brown sugar. Add eggs to creamed mixture. Add syrup and flavoring. Add dry mixture. Add walnuts. Drop by teaspoonful onto ungreased baking sheet. Put ½ walnut half on each cookie. Bake in 400 degree oven for 8 to 10 minutes.

Yield: 2 to 3 dozen, depending on size   Donna J. Aldrich

Pumpkin Cookies

1½ cups brown sugar, packed
½ cup butter or margarine
    (at room temperature)
2 eggs
1 pound can pumpkin
2 cups flour, sifted
2 teaspoons baking powder
1¼ teaspoons cinnamon
½ teaspoon nutmeg
¼ teaspoon ginger
½ teaspoon salt
1 cup raisins
1 cup pecans, chopped

Preheat oven to 400 degrees

Mix sugar, butter, eggs and pumpkin. Sift dry ingredients and add to pumpkin mixture. Blend well. Add raisins and pecans. Drop by teaspoonful onto ungreased baking sheets. Bake at 400 degrees for 12 minutes or until lightly browned.

Yield: About 6 dozen cookies   Cassie Simonds

Cornflake Macaroons

¾ cup sugar
3 egg whites
1½ cups corn flakes
¾ cup shredded coconut
1½ teaspoons vanilla

Preheat oven to 300 degrees

Beat egg whites until they hold a soft peak. Add sugar gradually, beating constantly. With a spoon, fold in cornflakes, shredded coconut and vanilla. Drop from spoon on a well greased pan far enough apart so as not to touch. Bake in 300 degree oven for 45 minutes.

Jim Littlefield
Oakland House, Sargentville

Grandmother Merrick's Soft Molasses Cookies

⅓ cup shortening
½ cup boiling water
1 teaspoon salt
¾ cup molasses
½ cup granulated sugar
1 egg
2½ cups sifted all-purpose flour
2 teaspoons baking powder
½ teaspoon soda
1 teaspoon ginger
1 teaspoon cinnamon

Preheat oven to 325 degrees

Place shortening in bowl. Pour in boiling water and add salt. Stir in molasses and sugar. Add unbeaten egg and beat well. Sift flour; measure and sift it together with baking powder, soda, ginger and cinnamon. Stir into mixture. Drop by spoonful onto greased cookie sheet. Bake in 375 degree oven for 12 to 15 minutes.

Yield: 20 to 25 cookies

William S. Cohen
U.S. Senate

Wine Suggestions

Soups: Bouillabaisse, or main course soups and non-milk fresh soups, require a dry white Pouilly Fumé or Muscadet.

Chowders: A Rhone wine or other medium dry white wine.

Salads: When served before the entrée, use a light white Chardonnay. Caution: the vinegar in the dressing may overpower the wine.

Pastas: When served with a meat or tomato sauce, use Chianti or Barbera; with a cream or fish sauce, serve Soave or Orvieto.

Stews: Main courses require a Burgundy, a Rhône, or a medium dry white wine. Less hearty stews need a milder red.

Fish: Use a Chablis with oysters. Clams, mussels, and shellfish salads are accompanied by a Riesling. For a delicate fish such as sole or trout, serve Chablis or white Burgundy. Fatty fish such as salmon or bass require a white Burgundy or a Sancerre.

Use Pouilly Fumé or Sancerre with smoked fish.

Serve a fine white Burgundy, Graves or Chardonnay with lobster.

Birds: Avoid the very sweet wines, and serve a Burgundy or medium dry white wine.

Roasts or Grills: With beef, serve a red wine, and the finer the roast, the more expensive it should be!

With lamb, serve a red Bordeaux.

When serving stuffed pork, serve a Beaujolais. With pork alone, use a Riesling or good red wine.

Ham: Burgundy, Sauvignon Beaune, or a dry sweet Gewürtztraminer are appropriate.

Steak: use the best red wine you can afford.

Desserts: Avoid wine when serving a dish with chocolate.

Fruits, including pies, require sweet wines. Sauternes, port or Barsac are suitable.

Cheese: Most dessert cheeses are strong flavored (blue, English Cheddar, or Stilton) and they call for a sweet or strong wine such as port or Barola.

Herb Suggestions

There is nothing more rewarding than growing your own herbs either in a garden or in pots. Here are some suggestions to add to your already favored combinations of foods and herbs.

Accent Herbs:

Basil: certainly the most important summer herb. A must with tomatoes or in a green salad.

Bay Leaf: soups and stews would tend to be a flop without a bay leaf. It enhances flavors but use caution as it has a pervading strength.

Chives: lend a delicate onion flavor.

Dill: gives a delicious touch to cold dishes, salads and fish. Use occasionally as a garnish in place of parsley.

Marjoram: more delicate than oregano and lends a delicate flavor to vegetables, meats, fish and poultry stuffing.

Mint: a must with lamb, peas, and beans, but try adding chopped mint to cut up fresh fruit.

Oregano (or wild Marjoram):   use in moderation. It is an Italian herb and therefore adds character to such recipes.

Parsley: any dish becomes elegant with a garnish of parsley. It should be used as completely as onions.

Summer Savory: similar to Thyme but slightly more delicate. Important in poultry stuffings and takes away the tinned flavor from canned beans.

Thyme: belongs to chicken, clam chowder (sparingly) and onions, but a slight sprinkling in cooked vegetables is delicious.

Pungent Herbs:

Rosemary: a good indoor plant but use in moderation in cooking. A few sprigs over a leg of lamb and in medley of onions, carrots, turnips and potatoes is delicious. Discard sprigs before serving.

Sage: very aromatic and must be used lightly. A staple in poultry stuffings and any food that seems bland.

Tarragon: good with chicken, lobster, or in a salad bowl. It is very popular in France.

Garlic and   the most widely used herbs. They add flavor, body and
Shallots: texture to soups, entrées and salads. Be careful, however, as these herbs can overpower one dish at the expense of the rest of the menu. Also, be aware of your diners' preferences!

Measurements

1 average lemon is the equivalent of 2 to 3 tablespoons

1 stick of butter is the equivalent of ½ cup

2 cups of sugar is the equivalent of 1 pound

4 cups of flour is the equivalent of 1 pound

4½ cups of cake flour is the equivalent of 1 pound

1 cup of raw rice (not wild) makes 3 to 4 cups cooked

2¼ cups of brown sugar equals 1 pound

1 pinch equals ⅛ teaspoon

1 teaspoon equals ⅓ tablespoon

1 tablespoon equals 3 teaspoons

4 tablespoons equals ¼ cup

1 cup equals ½ pint

2 cups equals 1 pint or 1 pound

1 cup cottage cheese equals ½ pound

1 tablespoon gelatin jells 2 cups liquid

INDEX

Order Form

The Maine Collection
Portland Museum of Art Cookbook
P. O. Box 6128
Falmouth, ME 04105

Please send me _____ copies of *The Maine Collection* at $18.95 plus $2.50 per copy for postage and handling. (Maine residents please add $1.14 sales tax per book.)

Name _____
Address _____
City _____ State _____ Zip Code_____

Please make checks payable to *The Maine Collection*.

All proceeds from the book will be used for restoration of the McLellan-Sweat House, Portland, Maine.

Order Form

The Maine Collection
Portland Museum of Art Cookbook
P. O. Box 6128
Falmouth, ME 04105

Please send me _____ copies of *The Maine Collection* at $18.95 plus $2.50 per copy for postage and handling. (Maine residents please add $1.14 sales tax per book.)

Name _____
Address _____
City _____ State _____ Zip Code_____

Please make checks payable to *The Maine Collection*.

All proceeds from the book will be used for restoration of the McLellan-Sweat House, Portland, Maine.